MOMMA MAY NOT BAKE THAT SHORTNIN' BREAD ANYMORE, BUT YOU CAN!

Tired of bland, super-refined
white bread in plastic bags?

Searching desperately for
a new taste sensation?

Then, get cooking!

You're only a few simple steps away from
plump, fresh, tasty, wholesome loaves of

YOGURT DILL BREAD
RUSSIAN BLACK BREAD
BEAN SPROUT HEALTH BREAD
WHOLE WHEAT CHEDDAR BREAD

There's no reason to settle for
what the local supermarket has on its shelves,
when you can start baking breads
like these just by opening this book.

D1559727

Bantam Cookbooks
Ask your bookseller for the books you have missed

BAKING
BREAD
THE WAY
MOM
TAUGHT
ME

MARY ANNE GROSS

Illustrations by the Author

BANTAM BOOKS
TORONTO · NEW YORK · LONDON

▟

BAKING BREAD THE WAY MOM TAUGHT ME
A Bantam Book / September 1979

ISBN 0-553-12815-9

Published simultaneously in the United States and Canada

Bantam Books are published by Bantam Books, Inc. Its trade-
mark, consisting of the words "Bantam Books" and the por-
trayal of a bantam, is Registered in U.S. Patent and Trademark
Office and in other countries. Marca Registrada. Bantam
Books, Inc., 666 Fifth Avenue, New York, New York 10019.

BAKING BREAD
THE WAY MOM TAUGHT ME
is dedicated

to my mother,
Anne Buckneberg Gross,
who taught me how to make bread;

to my daughter,
Antonia Anne Ferraro,
who loves bread and butter;

and to my husband,
Angelo Ferraro,
who complains about buying flour,
but loves to eat my bread!

Contents

Introduction

My mother baked bread twice a week, almost every week, when I was a child. She usually made whole wheat bread, a nutritious everyday bread. But occasionally she made other kinds—white, potato, oatmeal and raisin, among others. Before Christmas she always made a Norwegian *Julebrød* filled with raisins and flavored with cardamom.

All of the children in our neighborhood called her Mom. Ever cheerful, good-natured, optimistic and giving, she was the quintessential Mom. She often baked cookies, cakes and pies as well as bread. The children would always ask, "Mom, can I have some?" Naturally, she always gave them some. We would all be playing down the road, hundreds of feet away from the house, when we'd smell that wonderful aroma of baking bread and go running to my house and ask, "Mom, is it done yet?" If it was, we'd all put butter on hot pieces of bread that Mom would break off for us. What a treat!

When I was about ten years old I began to learn how to make bread under Mom's direction. When I was a teenager I made the family bread quite often so Mom could have more time to work on her novels. I usually made simple yeast breads then, in amounts large enough to feed a family of eight. Then came years of experimentation with all kinds of breads. Many of the recipes in this book are new and the others are my own variations on traditional recipes such as French Bread. These recipes, all of which have been tested at least once, are the best, the tastiest of the many breads I have developed over the years.

It is possible to learn how to make bread from books, but it is best to have someone teach you for there are so many little things one should know. Yet there are many children and adults who want to learn the art of bread making but have no one to teach them. And that is how the idea for this book came to me. "Let Mom teach them just as she taught me," I thought. And once you've learned how to make a basic white bread you can try the many other bread recipes in this book. I have written them in a simple to follow, step-by-step procedure so that beginners can easily make good bread.

I can think of no food that is more delicious, more satisfying than a good homemade bread. And making your own bread greatly enhances that satisfaction.

Mary Anne Gross
Yesterday's Village
May 1979

BAKING
BREAD
THE WAY
MOM
TAUGHT
ME

M.A.G.

Weights and Measures

A pinch = ⅛ teaspoon

1 tablespoon = 3 teaspoons

4 tablespoons = ¼ cup

5⅓ tablespoons = ⅓ cup

8 tablespoons = ½ cup

12 tablespoons = ¾ cup

16 tablespoons = 1 cup

1 cup = 8 ounces or ½ pint

2 cups = 1 pint

1 pint = 16 ounces

2 pints = 1 quart

4 quarts = 1 gallon

1 pound of butter = 2 cups of butter

1 stick of butter = ½ cup butter

4 sticks of butter = 1 pound of butter

1 pound of flour = 4 cups of flour

1 pound of sugar = 2 cups of sugar

1 ¼-ounce package active dry yeast = 1 tablespoon
active dry yeast

1 ¼-ounce package active dry yeast = 1⅝-ounce cake
of compressed yeast

Rind of 1 orange = 1 tablespoon orange rind

Rind of 1 lemon = 1½ teaspoons lemon rind

Note: I used an ordinary tablespoon and teaspoon rather than measuring spoons in the recipes in this book. But I used a measuring cup rather than an ordinary cup.

However, measuring spoons were used for the above exact measurements.

Make sure all measurements are level unless otherwise specified.

Baking Bread
The Way Mom
Taught Me

"Mom, can you teach me how to make bread some-day?" Mary asked after she finished her bowl of milk-toast.

"How about today? It's still early in the morning, and that's the best time to make bread. Bread always comes out best if we're fresh and energetic when we make it," Mom answered. "We're almost out of bread anyway, so I'd better make some today."

"No, I'd better make some. I don't want to watch. I want to *do* it."

"All right. You do it, and I'll watch." Mom was glad that she wanted to learn. Each week she baked enough bread to fill several large crocks for her big family. It was a lot of work, and Mary could help once she learned how to make bread.

"But you have to show me how," Mary said.

"All right. First I'll have to put some more wood in the stove so the house will be nice and warm. Bread dough rises best in a warm room," Mom said as she stoked the fire. "While I'm doing this why don't you get ready?"

"I am ready." Mary put on a big white apron.

"You'll have to pin your hair up so it won't fall in the dough. And you'll be putting your hands in the dough so they have to be scrubbed clean."

When Mary finished scrubbing her fingernails and

washing her hands she put on a scarf to keep her long blonde hair neatly tucked back.

"Now what do I do?"

"Let's see. We have to get all of the utensils ready. I'll rinse out the big mixing bowl with hot water so it'll be warm when we put the ingredients in it. And why don't you get out a small bowl for the yeast, a big mixing spoon, a tablespoon, a teaspoon, a measuring cup, a pastry brush, two loaf pans and a small pot. Oh, and some clean white dish towels and a small terry towel."

Mary lined up the utensils on one of the enamel-topped kitchen tables.

"Now let's decide what kind of bread to make, then gather all of the ingredients together. I took the butter and eggs out of the refrigerator earlier this morning so they'd warm up to room temperature in case I decided to bake today. None of the ingredients should be cold. Yeast works best with warm ingredients."

"I think we should make an easy bread," Mary said.

"That's a good idea," Mom said with a smile. "You can make a simple white bread to begin with. Then when you understand how to do it you can make the other kinds of breads."

Mom put a clean terry towel under the mixing bowl on the table. "This will help to keep the batter warm. When you make bread you have to be very careful or it won't come out right."

She wrote the ingredients for the white bread on a large piece of paper. "Here's a good basic recipe. Read it, then gather all of the ingredients. Don't forget the salt! Put them on the table near the mixing bowl and check them off on the paper so you don't forget any. And after you use each ingredient in the batter put it aside, on the other table, so you don't put it in the batter twice."

White Bread with Wheat Germ

2 packages active dry
   yeast
1 tablespoon honey
½ cup lukewarm water
1 cup hot milk
½ cup soft butter
1 cup cold milk
7½ cups unbleached
   all-purpose flour

3 eggs
2 teaspoons sea salt
3 tablespoons honey
1 cup wheat germ
2 tablespoons brewer's
   yeast

3 teaspoons corn oil
1 egg, slightly beaten
Sesame seeds

Yield: 2 loaves

After reading the recipe and gathering all of the
ingredients Mary said, "O.K., Mom, I'm ready to
begin."

"First you have to prepare the yeast," Mom said.
"Rip open two packages of yeast and pour the yeast
into this small bowl. Then add a tablespoon of honey
and ½ cup lukewarm water. Stir it a little, then put
the bowl on the table near the stove where it's warm.
If it gets foamy and bubbly after a few minutes it's
good yeast. If it doesn't do anything after a few minutes, then throw it out and use two new packages of
yeast."

"Why does the water have to be lukewarm?" Mary
wanted to know.

"Hot water would kill the yeast and it wouldn't get
foamy in cold water. Yeast needs lukewarm water to
make it come alive. Now let's heat a cup of milk in
this small pot."

Mary put the pot of milk on the stove. Mom dropped
a stick of butter (½ cup) into the milk and said, "Stir
the butter around until it melts in the milk."

When the butter was melted in the hot milk Mary
poured the liquid into the large mixing bowl. She
added 1 cup of cold milk.

Mom stuck her finger into the liquid and said, "It's
lukewarm now. It's just right. If the liquid is too hot it

will cook the eggs. Now put in 1 cup of flour so that it will be easier to mix the eggs with the liquid."

When Mary had mixed in the eggs and flour, Mom said, "Now add 2 teaspoons of sea salt. Not heaping teaspoons, just level teaspoons."

"What's the salt for?" Mary asked.

"Without salt the bread would taste flat. I'm sure you'll find that out some day when you forget to put the salt in. That's why it's a good idea to gather all of the ingredients before you start."

"Now," Mom continued, "mix in 3 tablespoons of honey to give it just a hint of sweetness. The honey also helps the bread stay fresh longer. And then add 1 cup of wheat germ."

"Why wheat germ?" Mary asked.

"Wheat germ is the best part of the wheat. It's very healthy for you. We're using white flour in this recipe which isn't as healthy as whole wheat flour. So we'll add wheat germ to the dough to make the bread more nutritious. It has a lot of protein, iron and B vitamins."

"Why do we need all of that stuff?"

"So you'll look good and feel good and have a lot of energy. Now, put in 2 heaping tablespoons of brewer's yeast. That has a lot of B vitamins, too. Too much of it would not be good for you, but 2 table-spoons is a good amount for this recipe."

Mary mixed in the wheat germ and brewer's yeast, then wondered, "Why don't we just use whole wheat flour instead of white flour if it's not so good?"

Mom answered, "It's easier to learn to make a white bread. It's lighter and rises more easily. When you get good at making white bread you can experiment with whole wheat, rye and all of the heavier flours. Mother told me that when she was growing up in Norway they usually baked rye or wheat breads for everyday use and only had white breads on holidays, like the Christmas *Julebrød*. Someday I'll show you how to make that. Now let's add the yeast."

"I already did," Mary said.

"Not the brewer's yeast. I mean the baker's yeast in that small bowl. It's very foamy now."

"What's the difference between brewer's yeast and baker's yeast?" Mary wanted to know.

"We put the brewer's yeast in the dough to make the bread more nutritious. But the baker's yeast is alive. It makes the bread rise. When we knead the bread the yeast mixes with the flour and air and a gas forms that makes the bread rise."

"Oh, the gas makes it puff up sort of like a balloon," Mary thought aloud, then said, "Now all we have to put in is the rest of the flour."

"Are you sure? Check the recipe. Make sure you put in everything else."

Mary began to read the ingredients aloud. "Yeast, honey, water, hot milk, butter, cold milk, eggs, salt, honey, wheat germ and brewer's yeast. Now all we have to put in is the flour, corn oil, beaten egg and sesame seeds."

"No," Mom corrected. "All we have to put in is the flour. The corn oil is for rolling the ball of dough in after it's been kneaded, and the beaten egg and sesame seeds are for putting on top of the loaves after they've risen."

Mary added 1 cup of flour, then began to measure out another.

"What are you doing?" Mom asked.

"I'm going to put all of the flour in."

"All 6½ cups at once?"

"Yeah. Then I can start to knead it."

"Oh, my goodness," Mom said with a laugh. "You can't do that."

"Why not?"

"It would be too hard to mix it all in at once, and it wouldn't be as evenly mixed. We put in only 1 cup at a time and mix it with this large spoon after each cup until the batter is smooth. We may not need exactly 6½ cups. We may need less or maybe even more. On rainy days when there's a lot of moisture in the air we may need more flour than the recipe calls for, but on dry days we may need less. You have to let the dough tell you how much flour to add. That's another reason why we add a little at a time, just enough to make a soft dough that's doesn't stick to your hands."

Mary gradually added the flour, mixing it in the dough well after each cup. When she got to the last cup she said, "It's too hard to mix. Will you do it?"

"No. You have to learn to do it. Take the spoon out now and use your hands to mix it. You can begin to knead it in the bowl. And when it's not too sticky you can take it out of the bowl and knead it on the table."

"That's the fun part," Mary said. She had watched her mother knead huge pans of bread dough twice a week ever since she could remember, and she was ten so that was a long time. When she had mixed and kneaded enough flour into the dough to be able to handle it without getting sticky hands, she put it on the lightly floured table and pretended she was kneading clay the way she learned to in school. She put the palms of her hands on the ball of dough and pushed it away from her, then she gently rolled it toward her with her fingertips. After doing this a few times she pressed the ball of dough to the right and twisted it around, then pushed it forward and rolled it back. She repeated this process over and over, adding a little flour to the table if the dough was sticky. She kneaded firmly and methodically and was careful not to rip the dough, because that would tear the network which the yeast was developing in the dough as she kneaded. Her teacher had told her, "Work *with* the clay, not against it." She remembered that and worked *with* the dough.

Even though she enjoyed kneading, after five minutes she was tired.

"Take a rest, then knead it a few more times," Mom said. "If it's not kneaded enough the bread will not be as light as it should be. Knead it until the dough is smooth and you can feel air bubbles in it. That shows the yeast is acting in it to make it rise."

"It's all done," Mary said after kneading it a few

more times. Her hands and face and apron were covered with flour and bits of dough.

"Very good." Mom felt it, then shaped it into a ball and put it in the large mixing bowl. "Now just put a teaspoon of corn oil over it and roll it in the oil a few times."

"What does the oil do?"

"It keeps the rising dough from sticking to the bowl."

After "oiling" the dough they put clean white dish towels on top of the bowl and a clean terry towel on top of the dish towels for extra warmth while the dough was rising.

"Should I put the bowl on the table near the stove?"

"Good idea. That will keep the dough warm and help it rise. But don't put it too close to the stove. We could let it rise on top of the stove if it were a gas or electric stove, but not on a coal and wood stove. It's too hot."

An hour later the dough had risen almost to the top of the bowl.

"Now it's time to punch it down," Mom said. "We can't let it rise too long or the dough will get sour."

Mary punched the dough down in the bowl.

"Punch all of the air bubbles out," Mom instructed. "You have to break up the air bubbles and spread the yeast gases throughout the dough so it will be light." Mom punched the dough for a few minutes to show her how.

After punching and kneading the dough in the bowl for about 5 minutes, Mary rolled the ball of dough in 1 teaspoon of corn oil, covered the bowl with towels and let it rise for another half hour.

"To make it really light knead it a third time," Mom said. "It isn't necessary. We could make the loaves now. But they'll be lighter if the dough is kneaded once more."

Mary punched and kneaded, rolled the dough in 1 teaspoon of corn oil in the bowl, covered the bowl with towels and let it rise for another half hour.

While the dough was rising Mary spread butter all over the inside surface of two 9x5x3-inch loaf pans. The butter would prevent the loaves from sticking to the pans as they baked.

When the dough was ready she cut it in half with a large knife. She had watched her mother shape loaves many times so she didn't need help doing that. Mary took half of the dough and folded it over and over, squeezing the air bubbles out, then tucked it in underneath and pinched the seams together so that she had a nice loaf to put into the loaf pan. She put the seam side down, of course, and she pressed the dough into all of the corners. The loaf filled the pan more than halfway up. She shaped the other loaf and put it in the second pan. Then she put the two pans on the table near the stove, covered them with a clean white cloth and let the loaves rise for about 30 minutes when they were almost double in size and the pans felt lighter. The oven in the wood and coal stove was nice and hot when the loaves were risen. If they had a gas or electric stove they would have turned the oven on right after shaping the loaves so that it would have had time to preheat to 350° F.

"Now you can mix an egg up in a cup and use this pastry brush to brush the egg on top of the risen loaves. It gives the bread a nice glaze. Then sprinkle the sesame seeds on top. They taste good and they're nutritious," Mom explained.

When Mary had finished putting on the egg and seeds she put the loaves in the hot oven. She wanted to peek in the oven after ten minutes, but Mom said, "No. Wait until the bread has had a good chance to bake and set. Let it bake about two-thirds of the way before you peek." After 35 minutes they checked to see if the loaves were done. They weren't brown enough. So they let them bake another 10 minutes.

"Are they done?" Mary asked.

"They look done and they smell done," Mom said as she peered in at the golden brown loaves. "But we'll check to be sure." She took a loaf out of the pan and tapped the bottom of the loaf with her knuckle. It sounded hollow. "They're done."

Mom took the loaves out of the pans and set them on wire racks on the table to cool.

Mary couldn't wait for the bread to cool. After five minutes she broke a crust off one of the loaves and let butter melt on it.

"Ummm. This is delicious!" she said.

Mom couldn't resist hot, fresh-baked bread either. "It's O.K. to break off pieces of hot bread, but don't cut it with a knife while it's hot or it'll be a little gummy." She broke off a big piece, put some butter on it, and after a few bites said, "You make good bread, Mary."

"Next time I'll make whole wheat bread," Mary said.

"All right. We'll go to the Mill and get some good stone-ground whole grain flour and you can make lots of different breads. We'll get rye and pumpernickel and soy and buckwheat. And we'll also get some oatmeal. Oatmeal bread is good. I'll write some of my recipes down for you and you can try them out."

"Which ones?"

"How about whole wheat bread, oatmeal bread, and potato bread?"

"O.K. I'll make those first. Then I'll make some recipes of my own," Mary said enthusiastically.

"That's a good idea," Mom said.

"I'll make peanut butter and banana bread," Mary said.

"What?" Mom laughed.

"Yeah. Peanut butter and banana bread. You know. Like the peanut butter and banana sandwiches you make for us. Only it'll be *in* the bread, not *on* the bread. Then all you'll have to do is take a slice.

"And then I'll make salami and cheese bread and then sweet potato bread and then grape bread," Mary continued. "Lot's of different breads."

"Oh, my goodness!" Mom laughed and her belly shook. "But maybe they'll taste good!"

"They will!" Mary knew they would.

Some Notes on Ingredients

GRAINS

I usually buy all of my grains at a grist mill in up-state New York where they are freshly stone-ground and free of additives. Stone-ground flours taste fresher and stronger than commercially-milled flours, so the breads made from them have a hearty, earthy flavor. You can buy stone-ground flour from health food stores but be sure it's fresh.

I keep my whole wheat flour and other heavier grains refrigerated so that they don't become rancid. But I keep my all-purpose flour in covered earthen-ware crocks. Flour can also be frozen.

1. *Unbleached All-Purpose Flour*

The bran and germ have been removed from all-purpose flour so it's not nutritious, but at least it's free of the chemicals used in bleached white flour.

Beginners should start with breads made with all-purpose flour because it has a high gluten content and is easy to work with. Gluten is what reacts with the yeast to make the bread rise.

All-purpose flour can also be mixed with low gluten flours, such as rye, in order to make high rising loaves.

2. *Whole Wheat Flour*

Whole wheat flour is made from grinding up the entire wheat kernel (bran, germ and endosperm), and thus it has all of the bran and germ intact. Many vita-mins and minerals and a lot of protein make it nutritious. It's high in gluten so it works well with yeast to form high rising loaves.

3. *Whole Rye Four*

Combine rye flour with all-purpose or whole wheat flour because rye flour contains very little gluten (the protein part of the wheat flour that reacts with the yeast to expand the dough). If you make an all rye bread it will be flat and heavy. Sourdough rye breads rise well and taste delicious.

4. *Graham Flour*

This is coarsely ground whole wheat flour.

5. *Semolina Flour*

Semolina flour is made from durum wheat. It is a soft, fine, faintly golden flour, which the Italians use to make a crusty Semolina Bread. Do not confuse semolina flour with coarse, gritty semolina.

6. *Barley Flour*

This is a fine flour that is rich in protein and minerals. Add a little to certain batters, or make a barley bread of barley flour and wheat flour.

7. *Buckwheat Flour*

High in B vitamins, this makes good pancakes and bread if mixed with whole wheat flour.

8. *Pumpernickel*

This is coarsely ground rye. It's very dark and heavy, and the only place I've ever found it is at the Tuthill-town Mill. I use a little of it in Pumpernickel and Russian Black Breads to give them that "rough peasant texture." Don't use too much of it or the bread will be heavy.

9. *Cracked Wheat*

This is coarsely ground wheat berries. Add a little to whole wheat flour or to all-purpose flour for a bread with a nutty texture.

10. *Cornmeal*

Cornmeal is made from dried whole corn that has been ground. I buy undegerminated cornmeal at the Mill, but you can get it at a health food store. Undegerminated cornmeal has the healthy part, the germ, left intact. It has more vitamins, minerals and protein than commercial degerminated corn meal.

11. *Rolled Oats*

Oats are rich in minerals and protein and give a nice texture to breads. Rolled oats are flattened oat kernels. I buy old-fashioned rolled oats, because the quick-cooking oats are tasteless.

12. *Raw Wheat Germ*

The germ is the most nutritious part of the wheat grain. It's the heart of the wheat, and it's the part that's removed to make white flour. It's rich in vitamins E and B, as well as in protein, oils and lecithin. Add ½ to 1 cup wheat germ to your breads for added nutrition. Keep wheat germ refrigerated or it will become rancid.

13. *Bran*

The bran is the outer layer of the wheat kernel. It's good roughage food and is rich in B vitamins and minerals. Add some to your bread for a more nutritious loaf.

14. *Soy Flour*

This flour is not made from a grain but from a legume; it's made from ground raw soybeans. Add ½ cup soy flour to your bread to increase nutritional value. Soy flour is rich in B vitamins, minerals and protein and is low in starch.

FATS

1. *Butter*

I use butter in some of my breads because I like its taste. I don't use margarine because it's made of saturated vegetable oils with chemicals added. Both butter and margarine are fattening, and it is better to use unsaturated vegetable oils (such as corn oil). So for everyday eating I make whole wheat breads with vegetable oil, but occasionally I make white breads with butter.

2. *Oil*

I use corn oil and peanut oil for the most part in my breads, although safflower and soy oils are also excellent. Unsaturated fats from pure vegetable oils are essential to your health. Among other things, they help to lower blood cholesterol, whereas hardened fats like lard and margarine contribute to cholesterol buildup in the blood. Check your labels. Many commercial oils have preservatives added. Refrigerate oil after opening the bottle.

LIQUIDS

1. *Water*

I use only spring water in my breads. That's because I have no choice. All we have is spring water, and we certainly appreciate it, especially after drinking fluoridated water in restaurants or other public places. My paternal grandfather, who was Italian, used to make a meal of dipping his home baked crusty Italian bread into the spring and eating it with some watercress that grows in the stream running out of the spring.

Use water as the liquid in your batters if you want to make crusty breads such as Italian or French breads.

2. *Potato Water*

When you make boiled or mashed potatoes save the potato water to use in your breads. It helps make high, large, light loaves. It also adds nutrition.

3. *Milk*

If you have children put whole milk in your breads for added nutrition. Milk is rich in calcium, phosphorus, vitamin A and protein. If you're on a diet use a substitute of powdered milk mixed with water. Milk makes soft, rich breads.

4. *Buttermilk, Sour Cream and Sour Milk*

Scandinavians use a lot of these liquids in their baked goods. My mother, who was Norwegian, often soured her milk to put in bread. These liquids produce a tender texture and help breads rise faster and stay fresh longer.

5. *Yogurt*

I often use yogurt in my breads. It's a very nutritious, high protein food which is easily digested. It manufactures B vitamins in the digestive tract and purifies the intestines of harmful bacteria. Yogurt and and milk are equally nutritious, but yogurt becomes the more nutritious one once it's ingested.

Make your own yogurt or buy the plain variety for your breads. Yogurt with fruit preserves is full of sugar and is fattening. Yogurt with chemical preservatives is junk food. So read your labels.

SWEETENERS

1. *Honey*

I buy unfiltered, uncooked honey from a health food store. Raw honey has more minerals than commercial honey. I use Wild Loosestrife Honey, which is dark and delicious.

Honey is a natural sweetener, and I prefer to use honey in my breads because it's not as harmful as sugar. It's also a natural preservative; it helps breads stay fresh longer.

2. *Blackstrap Molasses*

Blackstrap molasses is more nutritious than regular molasses. It's rich in B vitamins and iron, and it's a good source of calcium and potassium. It gives a great flavor and dark color to whole grain breads.

3. *Molasses*

Molasses is traditionally used as the sweetener in some Italian breads. It's not as strong tasting as blackstrap molasses.

4. *Raw Sugar and Brown Sugar*

These are both sugar with molasses added. I use them only when necessary such as in making a Cinnamon Roll. It's better to use fruit, fruit juices, molasses and honey as sweeteners when possible.

YEASTS

1. *Brewer's Yeast*

Add a little brewer's yeast to your breads because it is rich in B vitamins and high in protein. However, it is inactive; it will not make your bread rise.

2. *Active Dry Yeast*

This is a fungus, a live plant that makes the bread rise. It's rich in protein and has many vitamins and minerals.

Yeast produces a gas, carbon dioxide, which makes the bread rise when it gets trapped in the dough's glutenous network.

Yeast is killed if overheated and remains dormant when cold, so don't add it to hot or cold liquids. The liquid and batter should be lukewarm, if yeast is to work properly.

I use active dry yeast because it lasts a long time when refrigerated. But read the labels. Some yeasts contain preservatives.

If you live in a high altitude area (above 3,000 feet) you will need less yeast to make your dough rise. I live at the foot of a mountain, a low to medium altitude area. Adjust these recipes if you live up in the clouds.

I generally use about 1 package active dry yeast (1 tablespoon) for every 5 or 6 cups of flour. Heavier flours require more yeast.

SALT

I use iodized sea salt in these recipes. It's high in essential trace minerals and hasn't any of the unnecessary chemicals that are added to commercial salts in the supermarket.

Make sure the sea salt has potassium iodide added since iodine is necessary for healthy thyroid glands (which is to say healthy physical and mental development).

EGGS

Eggs are excellent protein food. Add whole eggs to breads for added nutrition.

Use yolks for color and to create light, soft breads such as brioche.

Brush eggs whites on top of risen loaves of Italian and French bread for a crisp crust.

Brush slightly beaten whole egg on top of sandwich loaves (bread baked in loaf pans) for a nice glaze.

CHEESES

Add cheese to bread for extra nutrition, as well as for flavor, texture and a moist loaf.

All cheeses are good protein food and are easily digested. But read the labels to be sure they are free of artificial colors and preservatives.

Cottage cheese and ricotta are particularly high in protein. Ricotta and cream cheese help make bread very light and spongy. Hard cheese such as Cheddar, Parmesan, Swiss and others are grated and added to bread for flavor.

NUTS AND SEEDS

Add nuts and seeds to breads for protein, minerals, B vitamins and unsaturated oils. They also add to taste and texture. Crush nuts or leave them whole in sweet breads.

Sunflower seeds and sesame seeds are particularly nutritious. Poppy seeds and pumpkin seeds are also good in breads.

BEANS AND SPROUTS

Beans and bean sprouts are rich in protein. Cook beans, mash them and add them to your batters. Chop up fresh, raw been sprouts and add to your breads.

HERBS AND SPICES

Add just a little to your breads for unique flavors. Cardamom is a favorite among Scandinavians, such as in *Julebrød*. Cinnamon is good with apples in bread. Herbs such as dill or summer savory are nice in cheese breads. Or combine your own favorite herbs in breads, but just a little. Don't overpower the bread with herbs or spices.

EXTRACTS

Vanilla, orange and lemon extracts are good to have handy for sweet breads. Vanilla heightens the flavors in breads. But get pure extracts, free of chemicals and artificial colors.

FRESH FRUITS, DRIED FRUITS AND VEGETABLES

Use berries, bananas, oranges, lemons, apples—almost any kind of fresh fruit in breads for flavor and nutrition. Use fruit or vegetable juices as a liquid in your batters. Dried fruits such as currants, raisins, figs and dates are good in sweet breads. Also use vegetables such as carrots, potatoes, yams and zucchini in breads.

NATURAL COLORING

Use one or two squares of unsweetened chocolate in Pumpernickel and Russian Black breads to make the breads darker.

Postum and Bambu are both coffee substitutes. Add a little of either powder to the batters to make dark breads such as Pumpernickel or Russian Black Bread. Blackstrap molasses also darkens breads.

Add mashed, cooked yams to make a golden yellow bread.

Mashed berries will also color breads.

My Concord Grape-Walnut Bread is purple, of course.

Soft Crust Breads

HELPFUL HINTS FOR MAKING SOFT BREADS

1. Use butter or oil, milk and eggs in the dough.
2. Honey will help to keep bread moist and fresh longer.
3. Brush an egg yolk mixed with milk or a whole egg on top of risen loaves before baking. Or brush melted butter on top of loaves before and after baking.
4. Bake at a moderate temperature (350°F. to 375°F.).
5. Store thoroughly cooled bread in an earthenware crock or in plastic bags in a bread box.
6. Add as little flour as possible, just enough to make dough non-sticky. This rules applies to all breads except for freestanding breads (those baked on flat baking sheets rather than in loaf pans) because they need the extra flour to keep their shape. Some Italian breads require extra flour and lots of extra kneading.

The amount of flour given in these recipes is only approximate and is subject to change. One day I may use 5 cups of flour in a certain dough. On another day that same dough (using the same recipe) may require only 4½ cups of flour. You must add a little flour at a time, using your judgment as you add.

Milk and Honey Bread

This is a light, high-rising bread, which is excellent for sandwiches.

1 package active dry yeast	8 cups unbleached
1 tablespoon honey	all-purpose flour
¼ cup lukewarm water	2 eggs
2 cups milk	3 teaspoons corn oil
¼ cup butter	1 egg, slightly beaten
⅓ cup clover honey	with 2 tablespoons milk
2 teaspoons sea salt	

Yield: 2 loaves

1. Combine yeast, 1 tablespoon honey and water in a small bowl. Set aside in a warm area until foamy and called for in recipe.
2. Heat milk until hot, letting butter melt in it. Pour into a large mixing bowl.
3. Add the clover honey and salt, blending thoroughly.
4. Add 2 cups flour, and beat for a few minutes.
5. When batter is lukewarm, stir in eggs.
6. Mix in foamy yeast.
7. Add 5 cups flour, 1 cup at a time, mixing well after each cup.
8. Knead 1 last cup of flour into dough on table or board. Knead about 10 minutes until dough is smooth, elastic and non-sticky.
9. Roll ball of dough into 2 teaspoons of the corn oil in bowl. Cover with clean towels and set in a warm area. Let dough rise for 1½ hours.
10. Punch dough down and roll in the remaining 1 teaspoon corn oil in bowl. Cover and let rise for 1 hour.
11. Form two loaves and place in two buttered 9x5x3-inch loaf pans. Cover with a cloth and let rise in a

warm place until double in bulk, about 30 minutes. Preheat oven at 350°F.

12. Brush tops of risen loaves with egg-milk mixture.
13. Bake for 35 minutes.
14. Cool on wire racks.

Oatmeal Bread

High rising and light, oatmeal bread is easy to make and good to eat.

1 package active dry yeast
2 tablespoons honey
½ cup lukewarm water
2 cups old-fashioned
  rolled oats
¼ cup soft butter
2½ cups boiling water
2 teaspoons sea salt

¼ teaspoon ginger
2 tablespoons blackstrap
  molasses
2 eggs
8½ cups unbleached
  all-purpose flour
2 teaspoons corn oil
1 egg, slightly beaten

Raw rolled oats

Yield: 3 loaves

1. Combine yeast, 1 tablespoon of the honey and lukewarm water in a small bowl. Set aside in a warm place until foamy and called for in recipe.

2. Put oats and butter in a large mixing bowl. Add boiling water and stir until butter melts.

3. Add the remaining 1 tablespoon honey, salt, ginger and molasses, blend thoroughly.

4. When batter has cooled to lukewarm, stir in eggs.

5. Add 1 cup flour and stir to blend.

6. Mix in foamy yeast.

7. Add 6½ cups flour, 1 cup at a time, mixing well after each cup.

8. Knead 1 last cup flour into dough on board or table. Knead for about 10 minutes until dough is smooth and non-sticky.

9. Roll ball of dough in 1 teaspoon of the corn oil in bowl. Cover with clean towels and set in warm place to rise for 1 hour.

10. Punch dough down and roll in the remaining 1 teaspoon corn oil in bowl. Cover with towels and let rise for 30 minutes.

11. Preheat oven at 375°F. Form three loaves and

place in three buttered 9x5x3-inch loaf pans. Cover with a cloth and set in warm place to rise for about 20 minutes, or until double in bulk.

12. Brush beaten egg on top of risen loaves and sprinkle oats on top.

13. Bake for 40 to 50 minutes.

14. Cool on wire racks.

Potato Bread

This is a light, high rising bread that is especially good for making sandwiches.

3 small potatoes
2 packages active dry yeast
2 tablespoons honey
½ cup lukewarm water
½ cup soft butter

8½ cups unbleached all-purpose flour
2 teaspoons sea salt
4 eggs
2 teaspoons corn oil
1 egg, slightly beaten

Sesame seeds

Yield: 3 loaves

1. Scrub potatoes and cook in water over medium heat for about 25 minutes, or until tender.

2. When potatoes are done drain and reserve potato water. Combine yeast, 1 tablespoon of the honey and water in a small bowl. Set aside in a warm area until foamy and called for in recipe.

3. Remove potato skins and discard. Mash the potatoes in a measuring cup (you should have about ⅔ cup mashed potatoes).

4. Put mashed potatoes and 1 cup warm potato water into a large mixing bowl. Add butter. Mash with a fork until butter is melted and mixture is free of lumps.

5. Blend in 2 cups flour.

6. Add the remaining 1 tablespoon honey, salt and eggs. Beat for a few minutes with spoon.

7. Mix in foamy yeast.

8. Add 5½ cups of flour, 1 cup at a time, mixing well after each cup. Knead 1 last cup of flour into dough on table or board. Knead for about 10 minutes until dough is smooth, elastic and non-sticky.

9. Roll ball of dough in 1 teaspoon of the corn oil in bowl. Cover bowl with clean towels and set in warm place to rise until double in bulk, about 1 hour.

10. Punch dough down and roll in the remaining 1 teaspoon corn oil in bowl. Cover with towels and set in warm place to rise for 30 minutes.

11. Preheat oven at 375°F. Form three loaves and put them in three buttered 9x5x3-inch loaf pans. Cover with clean towels, and let rise until double in bulk, about 20 minutes.

12. Brush beaten egg on top of risen loaves and sprinkle sesame seeds on top.

13. Bake for 40 to 50 minutes, or until golden brown.

14. Cool on wire racks.

Mom's Wheatena Bread

This is Mom's delicious, nutritious everyday bread. She used to make huge pans, 15 loaves at a time, but this recipe is for only 2 loaves. It's a moist, tender, high-rising wheat bread that slices beautifully and stays fresh for a long time. It is somewhat sweet because of the iron-rich blackstrap molasses.

2 servings cooked
   wheatena
½ cup cold milk
2 packages active dry
   yeast
2 tablespoons honey
½ cup lukewarm water
1½ teaspoons sea salt
3 tablespoons plus
   2 teaspoons corn oil

3 tablespoons blackstrap
   molasses
3 eggs
6 cups stone-ground
   whole wheat flour
1½ cups unbleached
   all-purpose flour
1 egg, slightly beaten
Poppy seeds

Yield: 2 loaves

1. Cook 2 servings wheatena according to package directions, using milk as the liquid rather than water (2 cups milk, ½ teaspoon salt and ½ cup wheatena). Pour hot wheatena into a large mixing bowl.
2. Blend in milk and let cool to lukewarm.
3. Combine yeast, honey and water in a small bowl. Set aside in warm area until foamy and called for in recipe.
4. Add salt, the 3 tablespoons corn oil and molasses to wheatena, blending thoroughly.
5. Stir in eggs.
6. Mix in foamy yeast.
7. Add whole wheat flour, 1 cup at a time, mixing well after each cup.
8. Stir in 1 cup all-purpose flour.
9. Knead last ½ cup all-purpose flour into dough on board or table. Knead for about 10 minutes until dough is smooth and non-sticky. (Only add as much flour as is needed to make a non-sticky dough.)

10. Roll ball of dough in 1 teaspoon of the corn oil in bowl. Cover bowl with clean towels and set in a warm place to rise until double in bulk, about 1¼ hours.

11. Punch dough down, and roll in the remaining 1 teaspoon corn oil in bowl. Cover with towels and let rise until double in bulk, about 1 hour.

12. Punch down, cover with towels and let rise for 30 minutes.

13. Form two loaves and place in two buttered 9x5x3-inch loaf pans. Cover with a cloth and let rise until almost double in bulk, about 30 minutes. Preheat oven at 375°F.

14. Brush risen loaves with beaten egg and sprinkle poppy seeds on top.

15. Bake for 60 minutes.

16. Cool on wire racks.

Note: Instead of topping loaves with egg and poppy seeds you can brush melted butter on baked loaves.

Oatmeal-Raisin Bread

Butter a thick slice of this bread for breakfast and serve it with hot cocoa.

2 packages active dry yeast	1 teaspoon cinnamon
3 tablespoons honey	2 tablespoons blackstrap molasses
½ cup lukewarm water	1 cup dark raisins, washed
2 cups old-fashioned rolled oats	2 cups stone-ground whole wheat flour
¼ cup soft butter	6½ cups unbleached all-purpose flour
2 teaspoons sea salt	2 teaspoons corn oil
2½ cups boiling water	Melted butter
2 eggs	Cinnamon
¼ teaspoon ginger	

Yield: 3 loaves

1. Combine yeast, 1 tablespoon of the honey and lukewarm water in a small bowl. Set aside in a warm area until foamy and called for in recipe.

2. Put rolled oats, butter, salt and boiling water into a large mixing bowl; stirring to blend.

3. When batter has cooled to lukewarm, mix in eggs, ginger, cinnamon, molasses, raisins and the remaining 2 tablespoons honey.

4. Blend in 2 cups whole wheat flour.

5. Add foamy yeast and stir.

6. Add 5½ cups all-purpose flour, 1 cup at a time, mixing well after each cup.

7. Knead 1 last cup all-purpose flour into dough on table or board. Knead for about 10 minutes until dough is smooth, elastic and non-sticky.

8. Roll ball of dough in 1 teaspoon of the corn oil in a bowl. Cover with clean towels and set in warm area to rise until double in bulk, about 1 hour.

9. Punch dough down and roll in the remaining 1 teaspoon corn oil in bowl. Cover with towels and let rise for 30 minutes.

10. Preheat oven at 375°F. Form three loaves and place in three buttered 9x5x3-inch loaf pans. Cover with a cloth and place in a warm area to rise until double in bulk, about 20 to 30 minutes.

11. Bake for 40 to 50 minutes. Then brush tops of loaves with butter. Sprinkle cinnamon on top.

12. Cool on wire racks.

Yogurt Dill Bread

This very light, fine textured, high rising bread tastes like spring! Serve it with potato salad and cold cuts for luncheon.

2 packages active dry
   yeast
1 tablespoon honey
½ cup lukewarm water
½ cup milk
½ cup soft butter
2 teaspoons sea salt
1 tablespoon dillweed

1 cup wheat germ
2 cups plain yogurt
4 eggs
8 cups unbleached
   all-purpose flour
2 teaspoons corn oil
1 egg, slightly beaten
Sesame seeds

Yield: 3 loaves

1. Combine yeast, honey and water in a small bowl. Set aside in a warm area until foamy and called for in recipe.
2. Heat milk in a small pot until hot, letting butter melt in it. Pour into a large mixing bowl.
3. Add salt, dillweed and wheat germ. Mix.
4. Blend in yogurt and eggs.
5. Add 2 cups flour, 1 cup at a time, mixing well after each cup.
6. Stir in foamy yeast.
7. Add 5 cups flour, 1 cup at a time, mixing well after each cup.
8. Knead 1 last cup flour into dough on table or board. Knead for about 10 minutes until dough is smooth, elastic and non-sticky.
9. Roll ball of dough in 1 teaspoon of the corn oil in bowl. Cover with clean towels and set in warm area to rise until double in bulk, about 1 hour.
10. Punch dough down and roll in the remaining 1 teaspoon corn oil in bowl. Cover with towels and let rise for 30 minutes.
11. Preheat oven at 375°F. Form three loaves and place in three buttered 9x5x3-inch loaf pans. Cover

with clean cloth and set in warm area to rise until double in bulk, about 20 minutes.

12. Brush beaten egg on top of risen loaves and sprinkle sesame seeds on top.

13. Bake for 40 to 45 minutes.

14. Cool on wire racks.

Challah

Challah is the Jewish egg braid. It's a light, delicious, beautiful bread that is easy to make.

1 package active dry yeast
1 tablespoon honey
½ cup lukewarm water
1 cup milk
¼ cup soft butter
2 teaspoons sea salt

6½ cups unbleached
   all-purpose flour
4 eggs
2 teaspoons corn oil
1 egg, slightly beaten
Sesame seeds

Yield: 2 braids

1. Combine yeast, honey and water in a small bowl. Set aside in a warm area until foamy and called for in recipe.
2. Heat milk and butter in a small pot over medium heat until butter melts and liquid is hot. Pour into a large mixing bowl.
3. Blend in salt and 1 cup flour.
4. Add eggs, beating with a spoon for a few minutes.
5. Stir in foamy yeast.
6. Add 4½ cups flour, 1 cup at a time, mixing well after each cup.
7. Knead 1 last cup of flour into dough on table or board. Knead for about 10 minutes until dough is smooth, elastic and non-sticky.

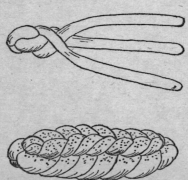

8. Roll ball of dough in 1 teaspoon of the corn oil in bowl. Cover bowl with clean towel and set in a warm place to rise until double in bulk, about 1½ hours.

9. Punch dough down and roll in the remaining 1 teaspoon corn oil in bowl. Cover with towels and let dough rise until double in bulk, about 1 hour.

10. Preheat oven at 375°F. Divide dough in half. Take one of the halves and cut off one-third of it. Cut the one-third piece into three even pieces. Cut the remaining two-thirds piece into three even pieces. With your hands roll each of the six pieces into long strips. Braid the three thicker pieces together, pinching the ends together. Braid the three thinner pieces together. Brush a very small amount of water on top of the fat braid and place thin braid on top of fat braid. Pinch ends of thin braid together with ends of fat braid underneath it. Place on a buttered baking sheet. Cover with a cloth and let rise until double in bulk, about 20 minutes. Repeat process with remaining dough for the second loaf.

11. Brush beaten egg on top of risen loaves and sprinkle sesame seeds on top.

12. Bake for 40 to 50 minutes, or until golden brown.

13. Cool on wire racks.

Sweet Butter Rolls and Loaf

A very light, mildly sweet bread with a spongy, cake-like texture, which slices beautifully.

2 packages active dry
yeast
¼ cup plus 1 tablespoon
honey
½ cup lukewarm water
1 cup milk
1 cup butter

2 teaspoons sea salt
1 cup wheat germ
9 cups unbleached
all-purpose flour
5 eggs
2 teaspoons corn oil
Melted butter

Yield: 25 rolls and 1 loaf

1. Combine yeast, the 1 tablespoon honey and water in a small bowl. Set aside in a warm place until foamy and called for in recipe.
2. Heat milk until hot, melting butter in it. Pour into a large mixing bowl.
3. Blend in the ¼ cup honey, salt and wheat germ.
4. Add 2 cups flour. Mix well.
5. Stir in eggs and beat for a few minutes.
6. Mix in foamy yeast.
7. Add 6 cups flour, 1 cup at a time, mixing well after each cup.
8. Knead 1 last cup of flour into dough on table or board. Knead for about 10 minutes until dough is smooth, elastic and non-sticky.
9. Roll ball of dough in 1 teaspoon of the corn oil in a bowl. Cover with clean towels and let rise for 1½ hours.
10. Punch dough down and roll in the remaining oil in bowl. Cover with towels and let rise for 1 hour.
11. Divide dough in half and form a loaf from half the dough. Place loaf in a buttered 9x5x3-inch loaf pan. Cover with a cloth and let rise until double in bulk, about 30 minutes. Preheat oven at 375°F. Bake for 45 minutes. Brush top with butter. Cool on wire rack.

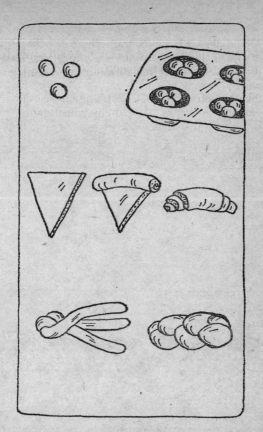

12. Make rolls with the remaining half of the dough. Divide into about 25 even pieces and roll into balls. Place in buttered muffin tins or on a buttered baking sheet. Cover with a cloth and let rise until double in bulk, about 30 minutes. Bake for 20 minutes, or until golden brown. Brush tops with butter. Cool on wire racks.

For Cloverleaf Rolls: Cut 3 walnut-sized balls of dough and place them together in 1 cup of the buttered muffin tin. Repeat until muffin tin is filled. Bake for 20 minutes or until golden brown.

For Braids: Roll out 3 walnut-sized pieces of dough between palms of hands until there are three long strips. Braid them, and pinch ends together. Bake on buttered baking sheet for 20 minutes or until golden brown.

Brioche

The many eggs in brioche make them very light and golden. Serve with some cheese and wine for a scrumptious little meal.

2 packages active dry
   yeast
4 tablespoons honey
¼ cup lukewarm water
¾ cup milk
1 cup butter
2 teaspoons sea salt

6¼ cups unbleached
   all-purpose flour
4 large eggs
4 large egg yolks
1 egg yolk mixed with 1
   teaspoon milk

Yield: 30 rolls, or 20 rolls and 1 loaf, or 2 large brioches

1. Combine yeast, 1 tablespoon of the honey and water in a small bowl. Set aside in a warm area until foamy and called for in recipe.
2. Heat milk until hot, letting butter melt in it. Pour into a large mixing bowl.
3. Stir in the remaining 3 tablespoons honey, salt and 1 cup flour, blending thoroughly.
4. Add eggs and egg yolks. Beat the batter well.
5. Blend in 1 cup flour, mixing well.
6. Stir in foamy yeast.
7. Add 3 cups flour, 1 cup at a time, mixing well after each cup.
8. Knead 1 cup flour into dough in bowl. Knead ¼ cup flour into dough on table or board. Knead for 10 minutes to form a smooth, soft non-sticky dough. (Because of all the eggs the dough will be a bit "wet," but not sticky. It almost feels oily after it's been kneaded. It's a beautiful dough to work with.) Place dough in a bowl and sprinkle a little flour on top.
9. Cover bowl with clean towels and place in sink filled with a few inches of hot water. Let rise for 1 hour.
10. Punch dough down and gently knead for about 5 minutes to get out all the air bubbles. Form dough

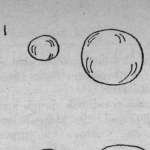

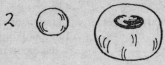

into a ball, cover and place in sink as before. Let rise for 30 minutes.

11. Punch dough down. Cover top of bowl with plastic wrap and refrigerate for 6 to 12 hours.

12. Remove from refrigerator. Knead dough on lightly floured table or board for about 10 minutes.

13. *To make 30 rolls:* Cut off one-third of the dough and set aside. Divide the remaining two-thirds into 30 equal pieces, form 30 balls and place each ball in a buttered muffin tin. Using the finger indent top of each ball a little. Form 30 small balls with the remaining dough. Dampen the indentations on the big balls with a little cold water and gently press the little balls into the indentations.

Cover with dry towels and let rise until double in bulk, about 40 to 45 minutes. Preheat oven at 350°F. Brush risen rolls with egg yolk-milk mixture. Bake for 25 minutes, or until golden brown. Cool on wire rack.

To make 20 rolls and 1 loaf: Cut off one-third of the dough and form a loaf. Place in a buttered 9x5x3-inch loaf pan. Cover with cloth and let rise until double in bulk, 1 hour and 40 minutes. Bake for about 50 minutes. Cool on wire rack.

Take remaining two-thirds dough and cut off one-third to make 20 small balls. Make 20 larger balls from the rest of the dough. Proceed as directed above for little brioches.

To make 2 large brioches: Divide dough in half. Cut off one-third of each half to form smaller balls and form two larger balls with remaining dough. Place smaller balls on top of larger ones (after indenting and wetting larger balls) in buttered brioche pans. Let rise until double in bulk, about 1 hour and 40 minutes. Brush with egg yolk-milk mixture. Preheat oven at 350°F. for 15 minutes and bake for 45 minutes, or until golden brown and hollow sounding when tapped on the bottom.

14. Cool on wire racks.

Sally Lunn

Sally Lunn is a very light, spongy, eggy, cakelike bread that is easy and quick to make because no kneading is involved. This is my variation of the batter bread which was developed in nineteenth-century England and sold by a young lady named Sally Lunn in the resort town of Bath.

2 packages active dry yeast
⅓ cup plus 1 tablespoon honey
½ cup lukewarm water
1 cup milk

½ cup butter
2 teaspoons sea salt
1 cup wheat germ
4 cups unbleached all-purpose flour
5 eggs, separated

Yield: 1 large loaf

1. Combine yeast, 1 tablespoon honey and water in a small bowl. Set aside in a warm area until foamy and called for in recipe.
2. Heat milk until hot, letting butter melt in it. Pour into a large mixing bowl.
3. Blend in the ⅓ cup honey and salt.
4. Stir in wheat germ.
5. Add 2 cups flour, beating for a few minutes with a spoon.
6. Blend in foamy yeast.
7. Add egg yolks. Beat batter well for a few minutes with spoon. (Save whites in a separate bowl.)
8. Add remaining 2 cups flour and again beat for a few minutes with a spoon.
9. Beat egg whites until stiff, then fold into batter and blend thoroughly.
10. Cover mixing bowl with a large inverted bowl (dough would stick to a towel) and place in a sink filled with a few inches of hot water. Let dough rise until double in bulk, about 1¼ hours.
11. Stir batter down and beat for a few minutes with a spoon. Cover and place in sink as before. Let rise for 30 minutes.

12. Pour batter into a well-buttered 10-inch tube pan (it will be about half full). Cover and let rise in a warm room for 20 to 25 minutes, or until almost double in bulk.

13. Place in cold oven. Set oven at 350°F. and bake for 45 minutes. Turn off oven and open door. Let bread sit in oven for 10 minutes with door open, so the shock of a sudden change of temperature will not cause it to fall.

14. Cool on wire rack or serve hot.

Two-Tone Bread

This is an unusual, fancy bread made by combining white and wheat dough in one loaf. There are many recipes for this type of bread, but this one is particularly light and tasty.

BASIC DOUGH:
2 packages active dry yeast
⅓ cup plus 1 tablespoon honey
½ cup lukewarm water
2 cups milk
¼ cup butter
2 teaspoons sea salt
3 cups unbleached all-purpose flour
3 eggs

WHITE DOUGH:
3⅝ cups unbleached all-purpose flour
2 teaspoons corn oil

Yield: 3 braids

WHEAT DOUGH:
4 tablespoons blackstrap molasses
5 cups stone-ground whole wheat flour
⅛ cup unbleached all-purpose flour
2 teaspoons corn oil

BOTH DOUGHS:
1 egg, slightly beaten with 1 tablespoon milk
Poppy seeds

1. To prepare the basic dough, combine yeast, the 1 tablespoon honey and water in a small bowl. Set aside in warm place until foamy and called for in recipe.
2. Heat milk until hot, letting butter melt in it. Pour into a large mixing bowl.
3. Stir in salt and the ⅓ cup honey.
4. Blend in 2 cups flour.
5. When batter has cooled to lukewarm, mix in eggs.
6. Add remaining 1 cup flour and mix well.
7. Stir in foamy yeast.
8. Pour half of the batter into a second large bowl (about 2¾ cups).
9. To first bowl add 2½ cups all-purpose flour, a little at a time, mixing well. Knead 1 last cup all-purpose flour into dough on table or board. Knead for a few

minutes. Cover with clean towels and set bowl in warm place until ready to knead dough again.

10. To second bowl add the molasses, blending thoroughly. Then add 4 cups whole wheat flour, 1 cup at a time, mixing well after each cup. Knead 1 last cup whole wheat flour into dough on table or board. Knead for about 5 minutes. Knead ⅛ cup all-purpose flour into dough, kneading another 5 minutes. Roll ball of dough in 1 teaspoon corn oil in bowl, cover with clean towels and place bowl in sink filled with a few inches of hot water. Let dough rise for 2 hours.

11. While wheat dough is rising go back to first bowl and knead the white dough for 5 minutes. Knead remaining ⅛ cup all-purpose flour into dough, kneading another 5 minutes. Roll ball of dough in 1 teaspoon corn oil in bowl. Cover with a towel and let rise in a warm area for 2 hours. (Whole wheat dough takes longer to rise than white dough, so we put the wheat dough in the sink with hot water to help it rise faster.)

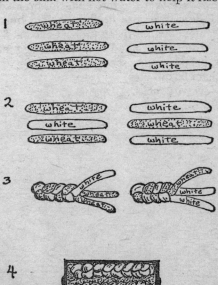

12. After both batches of dough have risen for about 2 hours, knead each one for a few minutes. Roll each ball of dough in 1 teaspoon corn oil in its bowl. Cover bowl of wheat dough with a towel and place in sink as before. Cover bowl of white dough and place in warm area. Let both doughs rise for 1 hour.

13. Divide both doughs into three equal parts. This will make three braids.

14. For one two-tone braid, take one piece of wheat dough and one piece of white dough. Again divide doughs into three equal parts.

Using your hands, roll each of the six pieces into 10- or 12-inch strips. (Handle as little as possible.)

Make two braids, one with two wheat and one white strip, and the other with two white and one wheat strip. Place the two braids side by side in a buttered 9x5x3-inch loaf pan.

Repeat the process with the four remaining pieces of dough, making two more braided loaves in 9x5x3-inch loaf pans. Cover the three pans of braided dough with a cloth and let rise until double in bulk, about 1 hour. While dough is rising preheat oven at 375°F.

15. Brush tops of braided loaves with egg-milk mixture and sprinkle poppy seeds on top.

16. Bake for 50 minutes.

17. Cool on wire racks.

Banana-Peanut Butter Bread

Many children love peanut butter and banana sand-wiches. This light bread tastes very much like those delicious sandwiches.

2 packages active dry
  yeast
4 tablespoons honey
½ cup lukewarm water
2 teaspoons sea salt
1 cup creamy peanut
  butter
2 eggs

3 large ripe bananas (2
  cups mashed bananas)
½ cup hot milk
2 cups stone-ground
  whole wheat flour
5½ cups unbleached
  all-purpose flour

Yield: 2 loaves

1. Combine yeast, 1 tablespoon of the honey and water in a small bowl. Set aside in a warm area until foamy and called for in recipe.
2. Put salt, peanut butter, eggs, bananas and the re-maining 3 tablespoons honey into a large mixing bowl. Stir until smooth.
3. Blend in hot milk.
4. Stir in whole wheat flour and the foamy yeast.
5. Add 4½ cups all-purpose flour, 1 cup at a time, mixing well after each cup.
6. Knead 1 last cup of all-purpose flour into dough on table or board. Knead for about 5 minutes until dough is smooth and non-sticky.
7. Cover with clean towels and set in warm area to rise until double in bulk, about 1 hour.
8. Punch dough down, cover with towels and let rise for 30 minutes.
9. Form two loaves and place in two buttered 9x5x3-inch loaf pans. Cover each with a cloth and let rise in warm area for about 20 to 30 minutes, or until double in bulk. Preheat oven at 375°F.
10. Bake for 50 minutes.
11. Cool on wire racks.

Sweet Potato Bread

This is a soft, fine textured, golden bread that slices beautifully and tastes superb!

2 large sweet potatoes
2 packages active dry yeast
3 tablespoons honey
½ cup lukewarm water
1 cup milk
½ cup soft butter
3 eggs
2 teaspoons sea salt

1 cup wheat germ
2 tablespoons brewer's yeast
4 cups stone-ground whole wheat flour
5 cups unbleached all-purpose flour
2 teaspoons corn oil
1 egg, slightly beaten

Sesame seeds

Yield: 3 loaves

1. Scrub sweet potatoes and bake at 375°F. until soft, about 1 hour.

2. Cool sweet potatoes until just warm. Peel and discard skins. Mash sweet potatoes to measure 2 cups and put into a large mixing bowl.

3. Combine yeast, 1 tablespoon of the honey and water in a small bowl. Set aside in a warm area until foamy and called for in recipe.

4. Heat milk until warm, letting butter melt in it. Pour into the large mixing bowl with sweet potato.

5. Add eggs, salt, the remaining 2 tablespoons honey, wheat germ and brewer's yeast, mixing well.

6. Blend in 2 cups whole wheat flour.

7. Stir in foamy yeast.

8. Add 2 cups whole wheat flour, mixing well.

9. Add 4 cups all-purpose flour, 1 cup at a time, mixing well after each cup.

10. Knead 1 last cup all-purpose flour into dough on table or board. Knead for about 10 minutes until dough is smooth and non-sticky.

11. Roll ball of dough in 1 teaspoon of the corn oil in bowl. Cover with clean towels and let rise until double in bulk, about 1 hour.

12. Punch dough down and roll in the remaining 1 teaspoon corn oil in bowl. Cover with towels and let rise for 1 hour.

13. Preheat oven at 375°F. Form three loaves and place in three buttered 9x5x3-inch loaf pans. Cover each with a cloth and place in warm area to rise until double in bulk, about 20 minutes.

14. Brush beaten egg on top of risen loaves and sprinkle sesame seeds on top. Bake for 50 to 60 minutes.

15. Cool on wire racks.

Cracked Wheat Bread

This is a light, high rising loaf with a slightly crunchy texture. It makes delicious sandwiches, especially peanut butter and jelly, which goes well with the crunchy texture.

2 packages active dry yeast
4 tablespoons honey
1 cup lukewarm water
1 cup milk
½ cup soft butter
1 cup plain yogurt
2 teaspoons sea salt
4 eggs

2 tablespoons brewer's yeast
2 cups cracked wheat
2 cups stone-ground whole wheat flour
7 cups unbleached all-purpose flour
2 teaspoons corn oil
1 egg, slightly beaten

Poppy seeds

Yield: 3 loaves

1. Combine yeast, 1 tablespoon of the honey and water in a small bowl. Set aside in a warm area until foamy and called for in recipe.

2. Heat milk in small pot, letting butter melt in it. Pour into a large mixing bowl and let cool to lukewarm.

3. Add the remaining 3 tablespoons honey, yogurt, salt and eggs. Mix well. Then blend in brewer's yeast.

4. Stir in cracked wheat and whole wheat flour, a little at a time.

5. Add foamy yeast.

6. Add 6 cups all-purpose flour, 1 cup at a time, mixing well after each cup.

7. Knead 1 last cup of all-purpose flour into dough on table or board. Knead for about 10 minutes until dough is smooth and non-sticky.

8. Roll ball of dough in 1 teaspoon of the corn oil in bowl. Cover with clean towels and set in warm area to rise until double in bulk, about 1 hour.

9. Punch dough down and roll in the remaining 1 teaspoon corn oil in bowl. Cover with towels and let rise for 30 minutes.

10. Preheat oven at 375°F. Form three loaves and place them in three buttered 9x5x3-inch loaf pans. Cover each with a cloth and let rise for about 20 minutes, or until double in bulk.

11. Brush beaten egg on top of risen loaves and sprinkle poppy seeds on top.

12. Bake for 45 to 50 minutes.

13. Cool on wire racks.

Anadama Bread

What a marvelous bread! It's dark, high rising and slices beautifully—a soft inside with a crunchy crust.

MUSH:
1 cup water
1 cup milk
½ teaspoon sea salt
½ cup undegerminated whole yellow cornmeal
⅓ cup butter

DOUGH:
2 packages active dry yeast
1 tablespoon honey
½ cup lukewarm water

1½ teaspoons sea salt
½ cup blackstrap molasses
½ cup wheat germ
2 tablespoons brewer's yeast
3 large eggs
2 cups graham flour
4½ cups unbleached all-purpose flour
2 teaspoons corn oil
Melted butter

Yield: 2 loaves

1. Prepare cornmeal mush: Heat water, milk and salt in a small pot until it comes to a boil; gradually add cornmeal, stirring constantly; quickly add butter, stirring constantly until the butter is melted and the mush is thick. (Constant stirring is necessary so lumps do not form. If they do, mash them out with a fork.) Pour mush into a large mixing bowl.

2. Prepare the dough: Combine yeast, honey and water in a small bowl. Set aside in a warm area until foamy and called for in recipe.

3. Add salt, molasses, wheat germ and brewer's yeast to mush, blending thoroughly.

4. When batter is lukewarm, add eggs and beat for a few minutes with spoon.

5. Add graham flour, mixing well.

6. Blend in foamy yeast.

7. Add 4 cups all-purpose flour, 1 cup at a time, mixing well after each cup.

8. Knead last ½ cup all-purpose flour into dough on

table or board. Knead for 10 minutes until dough is smooth, soft and non-sticky.

9. Roll ball of dough in 1 teaspoon of the corn oil in bowl. Cover with a hot, damp towel and place in sink filled with a few inches of hot water. Let dough rise until double in bulk, about 1½ hours.

10. Punch dough down and roll in the remaining 1 teaspoon corn oil in bowl. Cover and place in sink as before. Let dough rise for 30 minutes.

11. Preheat oven at 375°F. Form two loaves and place in two buttered 9x5x3-inch loaf pans. Cover with a clean cloth and let rise until almost double in bulk, about 20 to 25 minutes.

12. Bake for 40 minutes.

13. Brush tops of loaves with butter. Cool on wire racks.

Whole Wheat Potato Bread

This recipe makes two beautiful, high rising, tasty, dark loaves that are particularly good.

3 or 4 small potatoes
2 packages active dry
    yeast
2 tablespoons honey
½ cup lukewarm water
1 cup sour cream
½ cup butter
2 teaspoons sea salt
2 tablespoons blackstrap
    molasses

½ cup soy flour
1 cup wheat germ
3 eggs
6 cups stone-ground
    whole wheat flour
3 cups unbleached
    all-purpose flour
2 teaspoons corn oil
1 egg, slightly beaten
Sesame seeds

Yield: 2 loaves

1. Scrub potatoes and cover with water in a small pot. Cook, covered, over medium heat until tender, about 20 to 30 minutes. Remove potatoes and let cool. Reserve 1 cup potato water and keep warm.
2. Peel and discard skins. Mash 1 cup potatoes until smooth, then put into a large mixing bowl.
3. Combine yeast, honey and lukewarm water in a small bowl. Set aside in a warm area until foamy and called for in recipe.
4. Put reserved potato water, sour cream and butter in a small pot. Cook, stirring, over medium heat until lukewarm, then add to mashed potatoes.
5. Blend in salt, molasses, soy flour and wheat germ.
6. Stir in foamy yeast.
7. Mix in eggs.
8. Add whole wheat flour, 1 cup at a time, mixing well after each cup.
9. Add 2½ cups all-purpose flour, a little at a time, mixing well as you add.
10. Knead last ½ cup all-purpose flour into dough on table or board. Knead for 5 to 10 minutes until dough is soft, smooth, spongy and non-sticky. (Do not add too much flour for this is a soft dough.)

11. Roll ball of dough in 1 teaspoon of the corn oil in bowl. Cover with towels and let rise in a warm area for 1½ hours.

12. Punch dough down and roll in remaining 1 teaspoon corn oil in bowl. Cover with towels. Let rise for 1 hour.

13. Preheat oven at 375°F. Form two loaves and place in two buttered 9x5x3-inch loaf pans. Cover with a towel and let rise until double in bulk, about 20 to 30 minutes.

14. Brush beaten egg on top of risen loaves and sprinkle sesame seeds on top.

15. Bake for 50 to 55 minutes.

16. Cool on wire racks.

Rye Beer Bread

Rye Beer Bread is hearty and tasty.

2 packages active dry
  yeast
2 tablespoons honey
½ cup lukewarm water
1 (12-ounce) can malt
  liquor
2 teaspoons sea salt
3 tablespoons plus
  2 teaspoons corn oil
1 cup plain yogurt

2 tablespoons brewer's
  yeast
1 cup wheat germ
2 eggs
3 cups stone-ground rye
  flour
4 cups unbleached
  all-purpose flour
Melted butter

Yield: 2 loaves

1. Combine yeast, honey and water in a small bowl. Set aside in a warm area until foamy and called for in recipe.
2. Heat malt liquor until hot. Pour into large mixing bowl. Add salt, the 3 tablespoons corn oil, yogurt, brewer's yeast and wheat germ, blending well.
3. Stir in eggs.
4. Add 2 cups rye flour. Mix well.
5. Mix in foamy yeast.
6. Blend in 1 cup rye flour.
7. Add 3 cups all-purpose flour, 1 cup at a time, mixing well after each cup.
8. Knead last 1 cup all-purpose flour into dough on table or board. Knead about 5 to 10 minutes.
9. Roll ball of dough in 1 teaspoon of the corn oil in bowl. Cover with a hot, damp towel and place bowl in sink filled with a few inches of hot water. Let dough rise until double in bulk, about 1¼ hours.
10. Punch dough down and roll in remaining 1 teaspoon corn oil in bowl. Cover and place in sink as before. Let rise for 45 minutes.
11. Form two loaves and place in two buttered 9x5x3-inch loaf pans. Cover with a dry cloth and let rise

until double in bulk, about 30 minutes. Preheat oven at 350°F.
12. Bake for 60 minutes.
13. Brush tops with butter. Cool on wire racks.

Swedish Limpa

This is a big, high, wide, round loaf flavored with anise and orange.

1 package active dry yeast
2 tablespoons honey
¼ cup lukewarm water
¼ cup butter
1 cup buttermilk
1 teaspoon sea salt
2 tablespoons light molasses
¼ cup wheat germ
1 cup stone-ground rye flour

1 large egg
Grated rind of 1 orange
1 teaspoon crushed anise seed
2½ cups stone-ground whole wheat flour
1½ cups unbleached all-purpose flour
2 teaspoons corn oil
Milk

Yield: 1 very big loaf

1. Combine yeast, honey and water in a small bowl. Set aside in a warm area until foamy and called for in recipe.
2. In a small pot heat butter over low heat until it melts. Add buttermilk and heat until very warm. Pour into a large mixing bowl.
3. Add salt, molasses, wheat germ and rye flour, blending thoroughly.
4. Stir in egg.
5. Add orange rind and anise seed. Mix.
6. Mix in foamy yeast.
7. Add whole wheat flour, a little at a time, stirring as you add.
8. Blend in 1 cup all-purpose flour.
9. Knead last ½ cup all-purpose flour into dough on table or board. Knead for 10 to 15 minutes until dough is firm, smooth and non-sticky.
10. Roll ball of dough in 1 teaspoon of the corn oil in bowl. Cover with a hot, damp towel and place bowl in sink filled with a few inches of hot water. Let dough rise until double in bulk, about 1½ to 2 hours.

11. Punch dough down and roll in the remaining 1 teaspoon corn oil in bowl. Cover and place in sink as before. Let rise for 1 hour.

12. Preheat oven at 350°F. Form one round loaf and place on a buttered baking sheet. Prick the top of the loaf all over with a fork. Cover with dry towel and let rise until double in bulk, about 25 to 30 minutes.

13. Brush top with milk.

14. Bake for 50 minutes.

15. Cool on wire rack.

Oatmeal-Honey-Wheat Germ Bread

When we eat oatmeal we add honey, wheat germ and milk for a delicious cereal. My husband Angelo loves it, and he asked me to make a bread using these ingredients. So I did. It's soft, high rising and has a good texture.

2 packages active dry yeast
5 tablespoons honey
½ cup lukewarm water
2 cups old-fashioned rolled oats
1 cup boiling water
1 cup milk
½ cup butter
2 teaspoons sea salt
½ cup wheat germ
3 eggs
2 cups stone-ground whole wheat flour
4½ cups unbleached all-purpose flour
2 teaspoons corn oil
1 egg, slightly beaten
Raw rolled oats

Yield: 2 loaves

1. Combine yeast, 1 of the tablespoons honey and lukewarm water in a small bowl. Set aside until foamy and called for in recipe.
2. Put rolled oats into a large mixing bowl. Pour boiling water into bowl and stir.
3. Heat milk until just boiling, letting butter melt in it. Combine with rolled oats, stirring.
4. Stir in the remaining 4 tablespoons honey and salt. Cool to lukewarm.
5. Add wheat germ, stirring.
6. Beat in eggs with a spoon.
7. Add foamy yeast and blend thoroughly.
8. Add whole wheat flour, 1 cup at a time, mixing well after each cup.
9. Add 4 cups all-purpose flour, 1 cup at a time, mixing well after each cup.
10. Knead last ½ cup all-purpose flour into dough on table or board. Knead for about 5 minutes.
11. Roll ball of dough in 1 teaspoon of the corn oil

in bowl. Cover with clean towels and let rise for 1½ hours.

12. Punch dough down and roll in the remaining 1 teaspoon corn oil in bowl. Cover with towels and let rise for 1 hour.

13. Form two loaves and place in two buttered 9x5x3-inch loaf pans. Cover with a cloth and let rise until double in bulk, about 40 minutes. Preheat oven at 375°F.

14. Brush beaten egg on top of risen loaves and sprinkle raw oats on top.

15. Bake for 55 to 60 minutes. Use aluminum foil to cover top of bread after 45 minutes so tops don't get too dark.

16. Cool on wire racks.

Potato Oatmeal Wheat Bread

This is a very satisfying, tasty bread that is excellent for sandwiches. While baking, it makes the house smell so "homey."

2 cups water
2 teaspoons sea salt
1 cup old-fashioned rolled oats
½ cup butter
2 packages active dry yeast
2 tablespoons honey
½ cup lukewarm water
⅔ cup mashed potatoes

½ cup milk
4 eggs
½ cup wheat germ
4 cups stone-ground whole wheat flour
4¼ cups unbleached all-purpose flour
2 teaspoons corn oil
1 egg, slightly beaten
Raw oats

Yield: 2 loaves

1. Prepare oatmeal: Let 2 cups water come to a boil in a small pot. Add ½ teaspoon of the salt. Slowly add rolled oats. Lower heat to medium and cook, stirring, until oatmeal is thick. Pour into a large mixing bowl.
2. Let butter melt in hot oatmeal.
3. Combine yeast, honey and lukewarm water in a small bowl. Set aside in a warm place until foamy and called for in recipe.
4. Add mashed potatoes, the 1½ teaspoons salt and milk to oatmeal.
5. When batter is lukewarm, beat in eggs with a spoon.
6. Stir in wheat germ and then foamy yeast.
7. Add whole wheat flour, 1 cup at a time, mixing well after each cup.
8. Add 3 cups all-purpose flour, 1 cup at a time, mixing well after each cup.
9. Knead last 1¼ cups all-purpose flour into dough on table or board. Knead for about 5 to 10 minutes until dough is soft and non-sticky.

10. Roll ball of dough in 1 teaspoon of the corn oil in bowl. Cover with clean towels and let rise for 1½ hours.

11. Punch dough down and roll in the remaining 1 teaspoon corn oil in bowl. Cover with towels and let rise for 1 hour.

12. Form two loaves and place in two buttered 9x5x3-inch loaf pans. Cover with a cloth and let rise until double in bulk, about 30 minutes. Preheat oven at 375°F.

13. Brush beaten egg on risen loaves, and sprinkle raw oats on top. Bake for 50 to 60 minutes.

14. Cool on wire racks.

Refrigerator Rise Yeast Raised Corn Bread

This is a very close textured, soft, moist bread. It stays fresh for a long time and tastes just as good several days after baking it.

1 cup water
1 cup milk
2 teaspoons sea salt
½ cup undegerminated whole yellow cornmeal
⅓ cup butter
2 packages active dry yeast
4 tablespoons honey

½ cup lukewarm water
1 cup plain yogurt
3 eggs
1 cup wheat germ
3 cups stone-ground whole wheat flour
4½ cups unbleached all-purpose flour
2 teaspoons corn oil

Melted butter

Yield: 2 loaves

1. Prepare cornmeal mush: Heat 1 cup water, milk with ½ teaspoon of the salt over high heat until it comes to a boil; lower heat to medium and slowly add cornmeal, stirring constantly; add butter, stirring constantly until mush is thick and butter has melted. Pour mush into a large mixing bowl and smooth out any lumps with a fork. Let cool to lukewarm.
2. Combine yeast, 1 tablespoon of the honey and lukewarm water in a small bowl. Set aside in a warm place until foamy and called for in recipe.
3. Add the remaining 3 tablespoons honey and 1½ teaspoons salt, yogurt, eggs and wheat germ to mush, blending thoroughly.
4. Stir in 1 cup whole wheat flour, mixing well.
5. Add foamy yeast. Mix well.
6. Blend in 2 cups whole wheat flour.
7. Add 4 cups all-purpose flour, 1 cup at a time, mixing well after each cup.
8. Knead last ½ cup all-purpose flour into dough on table or board. Knead thoroughly for about 5 to 10 minutes until dough is firm and non-sticky.

9. Roll ball of dough in 1 teaspoon of the corn oil in bowl. Cover with clean towels and let rise for 1 hour.

10. Punch dough down and roll in the remaining 1 teaspoon corn oil in bowl. Cover loosely with plastic wrap. Refrigerate for at least 3 hours.

11. Knead dough for a few minutes, then form two loaves and place in two buttered 9x5x3-inch loaf pans. Cover with a cloth and let rise until double in bulk, about 1½ hours.

12. Preheat oven at 350°F. Bake for 50 to 55 minutes. Use aluminum foil to cover top of loaves after 30 minutes so tops don't get too dark.

13. Cool on wire racks. Brush melted butter on tops.

Refrigerator Rise Sour Cream Potato Bread

A light, tender, soft, moist, very high rising bread.

2 packages active dry yeast	2 teaspoons sea salt
2 tablespoons honey	6½ cups unbleached all-purpose flour
½ cup lukewarm water	4 large eggs
1 cup sour cream	½ cup wheat germ
½ cup mashed potatoes	2 teaspoons corn oil
½ cup butter	Melted butter

Yield: 2 loaves

1. Combine yeast, honey and water in a small bowl. Set aside in a warm place until foamy and called for in recipe.
2. Put sour cream, mashed potatoes and butter in a small pot over low heat. Stir until butter melts and liquid is very warm. Pour into a large mixing bowl.
3. Add salt and 2 cups flour, blending thoroughly.
4. Stir in eggs.
5. Add wheat germ and stir.
6. Add 4 cups flour, 1 cup at a time, mixing well after each cup.
7. Knead last ½ cup flour into dough on table or board. Knead well for about 5 to 10 minutes to form a soft, non-sticky dough.
8. Roll ball of dough in 1 teaspoon of the corn oil in bowl. Cover with towels and let rise in warm area for 2 hours.
9. Punch dough down. Shape into two loaves and place in two buttered 8½x4½x2⅝-inch loaf pans. Cover loosely with greased aluminum foil and refrigerate for 5 or more hours.
10. Preheat oven at 350°F. for 10 to 15 minutes. While oven is preheating let loaves sit at room temperature. Bake for 50 to 55 minutes.
11. Cool on wire racks. Brush butter on tops of risen loaves.

Crusty Breads

HELPFUL HINTS FOR MAKING CRUSTY BREADS

1. Omit fats and use water as the liquid rather than milk in the dough.

2. Brush loaves with egg white mixed with cold water before baking. But for crusty breads most similar to those you'd buy in an Italian bakery, omit the egg wash and simply brush salt water (1 teaspoon salt to ½ cup water) over risen, slashed loaves before placing loaves in the oven and brush again with salt water every 15 minutes. This creates the most wonderful crust.

3. Bake at a high temperature (400°F.) for the first 20 minutes, then lower temperature to 350°F. This produces a very crisp crust.

4. Brush loaves with water or salt water (1 teaspoon salt mixed in ½ cup water) every 15 minutes while they bake.

5. Bake in a dark pan.

6. Create steam by putting a pan of hot water on bottom shelf of oven.

7. Bake loaves directly on quarry tiles placed on bottom shelf of oven.

8. Build your own stone or brick oven outdoors for fantastic crusty bread.

9. Let cold air from a fan blow on hot bread right out of oven.

10. Store in brown bags. Do not store in plastic bags or crust will soften.

11. Store in refrigerator, although not for too long or they will dry out. But refrigeration keeps bread crusty. Do not store in crocks or a bread box or crust will soften.

Crusty French Bread

A delicious soft bread with a crisp, hard crust that is easy to make.

1 package active dry yeast
1 tablespoon honey
½ cup lukewarm water
1 cup hot water
2 teaspoons sea salt

4 cups unbleached
   all-purpose flour
½ cup wheat germ
2 teaspoons corn oil
Cornmeal for pan

Salt water (1 teaspoon
   salt dissolved in ½ cup
   warm water)

Yield: 1 large loaf or 2 long, skinny loaves

1. Combine yeast, honey and lukewarm water in a small bowl. Set aside in warm area until foamy and called for in recipe.
2. Put hot water, salt and 2 cups flour in large mixing bowl, blending thoroughly. Stir in wheat germ.
3. Mix in foamy yeast.
4. Add 1½ cups flour, a little at a time, mixing well.
5. Knead last ½ cup flour into dough on table or board. Knead 10 to 15 minutes until dough is smooth, elastic and non-sticky.
6. Roll ball of dough in 1 teaspoon of the corn oil in bowl. Cover bowl with a hot, damp towel and place in sink filled with a few inches of hot water. Let dough rise until double in bulk, about 2 hours.
7. Punch dough down and roll in the remaining 1 teaspoon corn oil in bowl. Cover with a hot, damp towel and place in sink as before. Let dough rise for 1 hour.
8. Knead dough a minute or two. Divide in two, if forming two loaves. Otherwise, for one loaf flatten dough on table with palms of hands, gently spreading it out in a rectangular shape. Press out all air bubbles. Roll up tightly lengthwise, pinching seams and ends together. Place loaf, seam side down, on a buttered baking sheet that has been sprinkled with cornmeal.

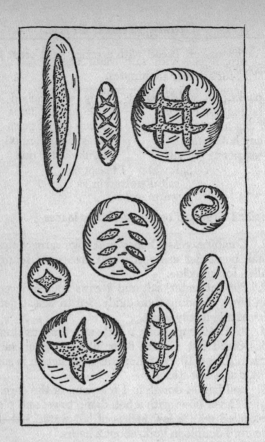

(Or use a French bread pan if you're lucky enough to own one.) Use a dark pan for a crisper crust. Taper ends of loaf. Cover with a dry towel and let rise in warm place until double in bulk, about 30 minutes. While dough is rising preheat oven at 400°F. Place a pan of hot water on the bottom shelf of the oven to create steam for a crisp crust.

9. Slash top of risen loaf three times across the width using a sharp, serrated knife or razor. Do not slash more than ½ inch deep or bread will fall (in which case you'd have to knead, reshape and let rise again).

10. Brush loaf with salt water.

11. Bake at 400°F. for 15 minutes.

12. Brush loaf with salt water again and bake at 400°F. for another 15 minutes.

13. Remove pan of water from oven and lower heat to 350°F. Brush with salt water again. Bake another 15 minutes.

14. Brush once more with salt water and bake a final 10 to 15 minutes. Total baking time is 55 to 60 minutes for one large loaf. Two long skinny loaves will bake more quickly. When done, they will be golden brown, crusty and will sound hollow when tapped.

15. Cool bread on wire racks with cold air from a fan blowing on it to crackle crust.

16. Do not store in plastic bag or in breadbox or the crust will soften. Store in brown bag in refrigerator to keep crust crisp.

Italian Wheat Bread

This recipe makes two big, crusty loaves.

2 packages active dry
   yeast
1 tablespoon honey
½ cup lukewarm water
2 cups hot water
3 tablespoons plus
   2 teaspoons corn oil
1 tablespoon light
   molasses

2 teaspoons sea salt
3¾ cups stone-ground
   whole wheat flour
4 cups unbleached
   all-purpose flour
Cornmeal for pan
Salt water (1 teaspoon
   salt dissolved in ½ cup
   warm water)

Yield: 2 loaves

1. Combine yeast, honey and lukewarm water in a small bowl. Set aside in a warm area until foamy and called for in recipe.

2. Pour hot water into large mixing bowl. Blend in the 3 tablespoons corn oil, molasses and sea salt.

3. Add whole wheat flour, a little at a time, mixing as you add.

4. Stir in foamy yeast.

5. Add 2 cups all-purpose flour, 1 cup at a time, mixing well.

6. Knead last 2 cups all-purpose flour into dough on table or board. Knead for 25 minutes until dough is smooth, firm and non-sticky. (Italian breads need a lot of kneading.)

7. Roll ball of dough in 1 teaspoon of the corn oil in bowl. Cover bowl with a hot, damp towel and place in sink filled with a few inches of hot water. Let dough rise until double in bulk, about 1 hour.

8. Punch dough down and roll in the remaining 1 teaspoon corn oil in bowl. Cover and place in sink as before. Let rise for 30 minutes.

9. Preheat oven at 400°F. Place a pan of hot water on bottom shelf of oven.

10. Butter two dark baking sheets and sprinkle with cornmeal. Divide dough in half. Punch down one half.

cover with towel and prepare later. See note at end of recipe. Flatten other half of dough on a board with your hands to form an 8x12-inch rectangle. Roll up dough tightly lengthwise and seal seams. Place loaf, seam side down, on baking sheet and taper ends.

11. Cover loaf with a dry towel and let rise until double in bulk, about 25 to 30 minutes.

12. Slash risen loaf with sharp knife or razor. Either make one long slash about ¼ inch deep along the length of the loaf, or make three short slashes across the width at a diagonal.

13. Brush slashed loaves with salt water.

14. Bake at 400°F. for 15 minutes.

15. Remove pan of water and lower heat to 350°F. Brush loaf with salt water. Bake for 15 minutes.

16. Brush again with salt water. Bake another 15 minutes.

17. While loaf is baking prepare the second loaf, cover and let rise as directed for first loaf.

18. Brush loaf one last time with salt water. Bake a final 15 minutes. Total baking time is about 60 minutes.

19. Cool on wire racks with cold air from fan blowing on bread to crackle crust. Do not store in bread box or crust will soften.

Note: As soon as you have put the first loaf in the oven for its final 15 minutes of baking you can shape the second loaf. But if you have a large oven you can do them both at the same time.

Italian Sesame Seed Bread

This crusty loaf is a perfect dinner bread.

2 packages active dry
  yeast
1 tablespoon honey
2½ cups lukewarm water
2 teaspoons sea salt
2 tablespoons plus
  2 teaspoons corn oil
6½-7 cups unbleached
  all-purpose flour

Sesame seeds
1 egg, slightly beaten with
  2 tablespoons cold
  water
Salt water (1 teaspoon
  salt dissolved in ½ cup
  warm water)

Yield: 2 loaves

1. Combine yeast, honey and ½ cup of the luke-warm water in a small bowl. Set aside in a warm place until foamy and called for in recipe.

2. Put the remaining 2 cups lukewarm water, sea salt, the 2 tablespoons corn oil and 1 cup flour into a large mixing bowl, blending thoroughly.

3. Stir in foamy yeast.

4. Add 5 cups flour, 1 cup at a time, mixing well after each cup.

5. Knead last ½ to 1 cup flour into dough on table or board. Knead 15 to 20 minutes until dough is smooth and elastic.

6. Roll ball of dough in 1 teaspoon of the corn oil in bowl. Cover with clean towels and set in warm area to rise until double in bulk, about 1½ hours.

7. Punch dough down and roll in the remaining 1 teaspoon corn oil in bowl. Cover with towels and let rise for 1 hour.

8. Divide dough in half. Roll out each piece with a rolling pin to form long rectangular shapes. Roll up lengthwise into long loaves.

9. Butter a large, dark baking sheet, and sprinkle sesame seeds thickly down middle length of pan.

10. Brush egg-water mixture on top and sides of loaf. Roll loaf over into seeds. Brush upturned side with

egg. Roll again in seeds, adding more as needed until loaf is completely coated with sesame seeds. Repeat this process with second loaf if your oven is large enough to bake both loaves at the same time; otherwise knead that dough down and shape it when the first loaf has been put in the oven.

11. Leave seeded loaf on buttered baking sheet and taper ends. Cover with a paper towel and let rise until double in bulk, about 30 minutes. Preheat oven at 400°F. Set a pan of hot water on the bottom shelf to create steam for a crusty loaf.

12. Use a sharp knife or razor to slash risen loaf three times across the width, not more than ½ inch deep or it may fall.

13. Bake at 400°F. for 15 minutes.

14. Remove the pan of water and lower heat to 350°F. Brush bread with salt water and place it on the middle shelf to bake another 15 minutes.

15. Brush bread with salt water again. Bake another 15 minutes.

16. Cool on wire racks with cold air from fan blowing on bread to crackle the crust. Do not store in plastic bag or in bread box or crust will soften. Store in a brown bag in refrigerator to keep it crusty.

Prepare the second loaf in the same manner. Shape it when the first loaf has been put in the oven.

Semolina Bread I

The Italian bakers in Brooklyn, New York, make a wonderful semolina bread in their huge brick ovens. I buy my semolina flour from them, but they will not give me their recipe. So I experimented and came up with this recipe and the following one. They are both crusty and very much like the bread baked on Knickerbocker Avenue despite the fact that I don't have a brick oven—yet.

2 packages active dry
   yeast
1 teaspoon honey
½ cup lukewarm water
2 cups hot water
2 teaspoons sea salt
¼ cup plus 2 teaspoons
   corn oil

4 cups semolina flour
4 cups unbleached
   all-purpose flour
Cornmeal for pan
Sesame seeds
Salt water (1 teaspoon
   salt dissolved in ½ cup
   lukewarm water)

Yield: 4 small loaves

1. Combine yeast, honey and lukewarm water in a small bowl. Set aside in a warm area until foamy and called for in recipe.

2. Pour hot water into a large mixing bowl. Add salt and the ¼ cup corn oil.

3. Blend in 2 cups semolina flour, then 2 cups all-purpose flour.

4. Add foamy yeast, mixing well.

5. Add remaining flour, first 1 cup semolina, then 1 cup all-purpose, then 1 cup semolina, and finally knead in last 1 cup all-purpose flour. Knead for about 15 to 20 minutes until dough is smooth, firm, elastic and non-sticky.

6. Roll ball of dough in 1 teaspoon of the corn oil in bowl. Cover with a hot, damp towel and set in a warm area to rise until double in bulk, about 1½ hours.

7. Punch dough down and roll in the remaining 1 teaspoon corn oil in bowl. Cover with a hot, damp towel and let rise for 1 hour.

8. Preheat oven at 400°F. Divide dough into four equal portions. Form four small, round loaves and place them on buttered, dark baking sheets, which have been sprinkled with cornmeal. Place loaves far enough apart so that they don't touch while rising. Cover with a dry cloth and let rise until double in bulk, about 25 to 30 minutes.

9. Slash tops of risen loaves with a sharp knife or razor to form a cross on top, no more than ½ inch deep or loaves may fall.

10. Brush tops of slashed loaves with salt water. Sprinkle sesame seeds on top.

11. Place pan of hot water on bottom shelf of oven. Bake loaves at 400°F. for 15 minutes.

12. Lower heat to 350°F. Brush salt water over loaves. Bake 15 minutes.

13. Brush again with salt water and bake another 15 minutes.

14. Brush once more with salt water. Bake a final 10 minutes. Total baking time is about 55 minutes. Tap bottom of loaf. Should be crusty and sound hollow when tapped.

15. Cool on wire racks with cold air from fan blowing on the loaves to crackle crust.

16. Store in brown bag in refrigerator. Do not store in plastic bag or in bread box or crust will soften.

Italian Semolina Bread II

This bread is so good it's addictive. It's a soft, golden loaf with a crunchy crust. You can buy semolina flour in Italian bakeries, but be sure to check the flour. I've been sold semolina that is coarse and gritty. Semolina *flour*, however, made from durum wheat, is as fine and soft and smooth as all-purpose flour, only it's slightly golden.

2 packages active dry yeast	¼ cup plus 2 teaspoons corn oil
2 tablespoons light molasses	4 cups semolina flour
½ cup lukewarm water	2½ cups unbleached all-purpose flour
2 cups hot water	Yellow cornmeal for pan
2 teaspoons sea salt	Sesame seeds

Salt water (1 teaspoon salt dissolved in ½ cup water)

Yield: 2 round loaves

1. Combine yeast, 1 tablespoon of the molasses and lukewarm water in a small bowl. Set aside in a warm area until foamy and called for in recipe.
2. Pour hot water into a large mixing bowl. Add the ¼ cup corn oil, salt and remaining 1 tablespoon molasses, blending thoroughly. (Do not use blackstrap molasses in this bread; it's too strong.)
3. Stir in 1 cup semolina flour.
4. Mix in foamy yeast.
5. Add 3 cups semolina flour, 1 cup at a time, mixing well after each cup.
6. Mix in 1 cup all-purpose flour. Knead last 1½ cups all-purpose flour into dough on table or board. Knead flour in gradually, but knead vigorously and continuously for 20 minutes until dough is smooth, firm and non-sticky.
7. Roll ball of dough in 1 teaspoon of the corn oil in

bowl. Cover with towels and let rise until double in bulk, about 1½ hours.

8. Punch dough down and roll in the remaining 1 teaspoon corn oil in bowl. Cover with towels and let rise for 45 minutes.

9. Preheat oven at 400°F. Place a pan of water on bottom shelf of oven. Form two round loaves and place them on a large, dark baking sheet that has been buttered and sprinkled with cornmeal. Cover with a cloth and let loaves rise until double in bulk, about 25 to 30 minutes. (Use a large enough pan so that risen loaves don't touch each other, or use two pans.)

10. Slash tops of risen loaves ½ inch deep in crisscross fashion or make two parallel slashes with sharp knife or razor.

11. Brush loaves with salt-water. Sprinkle sesame seeds on top.

12. Bake at 400°F. for 15 minutes.

13. Remove pan of water and lower heat to 350°F. Brush bread with salt water and bake 15 minutes longer.

14. Brush with salt water again. Bake another 20 minutes.

15. Cool on wire racks with cold air from fan blowing on bread to crackle crust.

Crusty Italian Sausage Pepper Ring

This bread is for sausage lovers. Buy fresh, loose sausage from an Italian delicatessen for this bread. Serve this with cheese and wine or with spaghetti and a salad.

2 pounds loose sausage	¾ teaspoon black pepper
2 packages active dry yeast	2 tablespoons plus 2 teaspoons corn oil
1 tablespoon light molasses	4 cups semolina flour
½ cup lukewarm water	2 large eggs
2 cups hot water	4½ cups unbleached all-purpose flour
1 teaspoon sea salt	Cornmeal for the pan

Salt water (1 teaspoon salt dissolved in ½ cup water)

Yield: 2 rings

1. Fry sausage until well done, cutting it into small pieces as it fries. Drain on paper towels.
2. Combine yeast, molasses and lukewarm water in a small bowl. Set aside in a warm area until foamy and called for in recipe.
3. Pour hot water into a large mixing bowl. Add salt, pepper, the 2 tablespoons corn oil and 2 cups semolina flour, blending thoroughly.
4. Mix in foamy yeast.
5. Stir in 2 cups semolina flour.
6. Beat in eggs with a spoon.
7. Add sausage.
8. Add 4 cups all-purpose flour, 1 cup at a time, mixing well after each cup.
9. Knead last ½ cup flour into dough on table or board. Knead vigorously for 20 to 25 minutes until dough is smooth, firm and non-sticky.
10. Roll ball of dough in 1 teaspoon of the corn oil in bowl. Cover with clean towels and set in a warm area to rise until double in bulk, about 1 hour.

11. Punch dough down and roll in the remaining 1 teaspoon corn oil. Cover and let rise for 45 minutes.

12. Preheat oven at 400°F. Divide dough in half, and form into two rings. To form a ring, roll half of the dough into a 24-inch rope, using your hands. Then twist the rope around and around and join the two ends by pinching the dough together. Place the ring on a buttered baking sheet that has been sprinkled with cornmeal. Gently push ring in a little so it is smaller and closer together. Cover with clean cloth and let rise until double in bulk, about 30 minutes.

13. Brush risen ring with salt water.

14. Bake at 400°F. for 15 minutes with a pan of hot water on the bottom shelf.

15. Remove the pan of water and lower the heat to 350°F. Brush ring with salt water and bake for 15 minutes.

16. Brush salt water on ring. Bake another 20 minutes.

17. Cool on wire rack with cold air from fan blowing on bread to crackle crust.

Note: Prepare the second ring in same manner as first as soon as the first ring is about half baked.

Store in the refrigerator to keep it crusty. Do not store in breadbox or crust will soften.

A Simple Crusty Rye Loaf

This is a high-rising, freestanding loaf with a soft interior and a crisp, crackly crust. It's easy and inexpensive to make and is superb for rye toast.

1 package active dry yeast
1 tablespoon honey
¼ cup lukewarm water
¾ cup hot water
2 tablespoons plus
   2 teaspoons corn oil
1 teaspoon sea salt

1¾ cups stone-ground
   rye flour
2¾ cups unbleached
   all-purpose flour
Cornmeal for pan
1 egg white mixed with
   1 tablespoon cold water

Salt water (1 teaspoon
   salt dissolved in ½ cup
   water)

Yield: 1 loaf

1. Combine yeast, honey and lukewarm water in a small bowl. Set aside in a warm area until foamy and called for in recipe.
2. Pour hot water into large mixing bowl. Add the 2 tablespoons corn oil and salt.
3. Blend in 1 cup rye flour.
4. Stir in 1 cup all-purpose flour.
5. Add foamy yeast and mix.
6. Add ¾ cup rye flour, then 1 cup all-purpose flour, mixing well after each addition.
7. Knead last ¾ cup all-purpose flour into dough on table or board. Knead vigorously for about 10 minutes until dough is smooth, firm and non-sticky.
8. Roll ball of dough in 1 teaspoon of the corn oil in bowl. Cover bowl with a hot, damp towel and place in sink filled with a few inches of hot water. Let dough rise until double in bulk, about 1¼ hours.
9. Punch dough down and roll in the remaining 1 teaspoon corn oil in bowl. Cover with a hot, damp towel and place in sink as before. Let dough rise for 30 minutes.

10. Preheat oven at 400°F. Place a pan of hot water on bottom shelf of oven to create steam. Form one oblong loaf and place on buttered baking sheet that has been sprinkled with cornmeal. Cover with a dry towel and let rise until double in bulk, about 15 to 20 minutes.

11. Using a sharp knife or razor, slash top of loaf twice across the width, no more than ½ inch deep. Brush egg white-water mixture on top of slashed loaf.

12. Bake at 400°F. for 15 minutes.

13. Remove pan of water and lower heat to 350°F. Brush loaf with salt water and bake 15 minutes.

14. Brush again with salt water. Bake another 25 minutes. Total baking time is about 55 minutes.

15. Cool on wire rack with cold air from fan blowing on bread to crackle crust.

16. Store in brown bag in refrigerator.

Crusty Rye Bread

This is a light, crusty, high-rising rye bread.

2 packages active dry
yeast
1 tablespoon honey
2 cups lukewarm water
2 teaspoons sea salt
2 eggs
¼ cup plus 2 teaspoons
corn oil
1 tablespoon orange
extract

3 cups stone-ground
rye flour
3¾ cups unbleached
all-purpose flour
1 egg white mixed with
1 tablespoon water and
½ teaspoon salt
Cornmeal for pan

Yield: 2 loaves

1. Combine yeast, honey and water in a small bowl. Set aside in a warm area until foamy and called for in recipe.
2. Combine salt, eggs, the ¼ cup corn oil and orange extract in a large mixing bowl.
3. Mix in 1 cup rye flour.
4. Add foamy yeast. Mix.
5. Stir in 2 cups rye flour.
6. Add 3 cups all-purpose flour, 1 cup at a time, mixing well after each cup.
7. Knead last ¾ cup all-purpose flour into dough on table or board. Knead for about 10 minutes until dough is smooth and non-sticky.
8. Roll ball of dough in 1 teaspoon of the corn oil in bowl. Cover with clear towels and let rise in warm place for 1 hour.
9. Punch dough down and roll in the remaining 1 teaspoon corn oil in bowl. Cover with towels and let rise for 30 minutes.
10. Preheat oven at 375°F. Shape two round or oblong loaves and place on a buttered cornmeal sprinkled baking sheet. Cover with a cloth and let rise until double in bulk, about 30 minutes.

11. Brush egg white mixture over risen loaves.
12. Place pan of hot water on bottom shelf of oven to create steam to make loaves crusty.
13. Bake loaves for about 1 hour.
14. Cool on wire racks.

Buttermilk Rye Bread

This is a soft, high rising, fine-textured bread with a crisp crust—a big, round, puffed up bread. It's delicious with butter, a big chunk of Gouda cheese and a glass of milk.

1 package active dry yeast
1 tablespoon honey
¼ cup lukewarm water
1 cup buttermilk
3 tablespoons butter
1 tablespoon blackstrap molasses
1 teaspoon sea salt
¼ cup wheat germ
1 egg yolk

1¼ cups stone-ground rye flour
2½ cups unbleached all-purpose flour
2 teaspoons corn oil
Cornmeal for pan
1 egg white mixed with 1 tablespoon water and ½ teaspoon salt

Yield: 1 large round loaf

1. Combine yeast, honey and water in a small bowl. Set aside in a warm area until foamy and called for in recipe.
2. Heat buttermilk until warm, letting butter melt in it. Pour into a large mixing bowl.
3. Blend in molasses, salt, wheat germ and egg yolk. (Reserve egg white for brushing on top of loaf.)
4. Add rye flour, mixing well.
5. Mix in foamy yeast.
6. Add 2 cups all-purpose flour, 1 cup at a time, mixing well after each cup.
7. Knead last ½ cup all-purpose flour into dough on table or board. Knead 10 to 15 minutes until dough is smooth, firm and non-sticky.
8. Roll ball of dough in 1 teaspoon of the corn oil in bowl. Cover with a hot, damp towel and place bowl in sink filled with a few inches of hot water. Let dough rise until double in bulk, about 1½ hours.
9. Punch dough down and roll in the remaining 1 teaspoon corn oil in bowl. Cover and place in sink as before. Let rise for 45 minutes.

10. Preheat oven at 375°F. Shape a round loaf and place on a buttered dark baking sheet on which corn-meal has been sprinkled. Cover with a dry towel and let rise until double in bulk, about 20 minutes.

11. Using a sharp, serrated knife or razor, slash top of risen loaf in a crisscross, not more than ½ inch deep and 3 or 4 inches long per slash.

12. Brush risen loaf with egg white-water-salt mixture.

13. Bake for 40 minutes. Cool on wire rack with cold air from fan blowing on bread to crackle crust.

Pumpernickel Bread

This pumpernickel bread is dark and hearty.

3 packages active dry
  yeast
1 tablespoon honey
½ cup lukewarm water
2 cups milk
¼ cup butter
2 teaspoons sea salt
1 tablespoon Bambu or
  Postum
2 tablespoons brewer's
  yeast
6 tablespoons blackstrap
  molasses
1 cup stone-ground
  pumpernickel flour
  (coarsely ground rye)

1 cup stone-ground rye
  flour
3 cups stone-ground
  whole wheat flour
3¾ cups unbleached
  all-purpose flour
2 teaspoons corn oil
1 egg white mixed with
  1 tablespoon water and
  ½ teaspoon salt
Poppy seeds
Yellow cornmeal for pan

Yield: 2 loaves

1. Combine yeast, honey and water in a small bowl. Set aside in a warm area until foamy and called for in recipe.

2. Heat milk until hot, letting butter melt in it. Pour into a large mixing bowl.

3. Blend in salt, Bambu or Postum, brewer's yeast and molasses.

4. Add pumpernickel and rye flours, mixing well.

5. Stir in 1 cup whole wheat flour.

6. Mix in foamy yeast.

7. Blend in 2 cups whole wheat flour.

8. Add 3 cups all-purpose flour, 1 cup at a time, mixing well after each cup.

9. Knead last ¾ cup all-purpose flour into dough on table or board. Knead for about 10 minutes until dough is smooth, firm, elastic and non-sticky.

10. Roll ball of dough in 1 teaspoon of the corn oil in bowl. Cover with a hot, damp towel and place bowl in

sink filled with a few inches of hot water. Let dough rise until double in bulk, about 1½ hours.

11. Punch dough down. Knead a few minutes. Roll ball of dough in the remaining 1 teaspoon corn oil in bowl. Cover and place in sink as before. Let dough rise for 1 hour.

12. Divide dough in half. Flatten each half with your hands, then roll each piece up tightly into an oblong loaf. Pinch seams together, and place on buttered cornmeal sprinkled baking sheet, seam side down. Cover with a cloth and let rise until double in bulk, about 50 minutes. While loaves rise preheat oven at 375°F.

13. With a sharp knife or razor, slash tops of risen loaves three times across the width of each loaf, ¼ inch deep.

14. Brush tops of risen loaves with egg white mixture and sprinkle poppy seeds on top.

15. Bake for 50 to 60 minutes.

16. Cool on wire rack with cold air from fan blowing on bread.

Russian Black Bread

I experimented with many ways of making Russian Black Bread before being satisfied with this recipe. It is a light, high-rising, round, freestanding loaf. The color is very dark, the crust is very crisp and the taste is fantastic.

1 medium-sized potato
2 packages active dry
  yeast
1 tablespoon honey
¼ cup undegerminated
  whole yellow cornmeal
¼ cup wheat germ
1 square (ounce)
  unsweetened chocolate
1 tablespoon Postum
⅛ cup plus 2 teaspoons
  corn oil
¼ cup blackstrap
  molasses
1 teaspoon sea salt
½ cup pumpernickel flour
  (coarsely ground rye)

½ cup rye flour
1 medium-sized onion,
  minced
1 teaspoon butter
4 cups unbleached
  all-purpose flour
Cornmeal for pan
1 tablespoon Postum
  mixed with 3 table-
  spoons water
1 egg white combined
  with 3 tablespoons
  water and ½ teaspoon
  salt

Yield: 2 round loaves

1. Scrub potato and put it in a small pot with 2½-3 cups water. Cook until tender, about 20 minutes. Remove potato, peel and discard skin. *Save the potato water.* Mash potato to measure ½ cup. Put in a large mixing bowl with ¾ cup hot potato water.

2. Combine yeast, honey and ½ cup lukewarm potato water in a small bowl. Set aside until foamy and called for in recipe.

3. Blend cornmeal and wheat germ with mashed potato.

4. Melt chocolate in ¼ cup potato water in a small pot over low heat. Stir into batter.

5. Blend in Postum.

6. Add the ⅛ cup corn oil and molasses. Stir.

7. Add salt, and pumpernickel and rye flours, blending thoroughly.

8. Mix in foamy yeast.

9. Stir in 1 cup all-purpose flour.

10. Sauté onion in butter in a small skillet. Blend into batter.

11. Add 2 cups all-purpose flour, 1 cup at a time, mixing well after each cup.

12. Knead last 1 cup all-purpose flour into dough on table or board. Knead for about 15 minutes until dough is smooth, firm and non-sticky.

13. Roll ball of dough in 1 teaspoon of the corn oil in bowl. Cover bowl with a hot, damp towel and place in sink filled with a few inches of hot water. Let dough rise until double in bulk, about 1 hour.

14. Punch dough down and roll in the remaining 1 teaspoon corn oil in bowl. Cover with a hot, damp towel and place in sink as before. Let rise for 30 minutes.

15. Preheat oven at 375°F. Punch dough down. Form two round loaves and place in two buttered 9-inch round cake pans, which have been sprinkled with cornmeal (use low rimmed pans). Cover with a dry cloth and let rise until almost double in bulk, about 30 minutes.

16. Brush tops of risen loaves with Postum-water mixture.

17. Glaze tops with egg white-water-salt mixture.

18. Bake for 50 to 55 minutes.

19. Cool on wire racks.

Peasant Bread

A good, hearty, dark bread that is the perfect accompaniment to soups and stews.

2 packages active dry
   yeast
1 tablespoon honey
½ cup lukewarm water
1 cup milk
½ cup undegerminated
   whole yellow cornmeal
5 tablespoons blackstrap
   molasses
2 teaspoons sea salt
¼ teaspoon ginger

3 tablespoons plus
   2 teaspoons corn oil
½ cup wheat germ
3 large eggs
1 cup stone-ground rye
   flour
3 cups stone-ground
   whole wheat flour
1¾ cups unbleached
   all-purpose flour
Yellow cornmeal for pan

Yield: 2 loaves

1. Combine yeast, honey and water in a small bowl. Set aside in a warm area until foamy and called for in recipe.
2. Heat milk until hot. Pour into a large mixing bowl. Add cornmeal.
3. Mix in molasses, salt, ginger, the 3 tablespoons corn oil, wheat germ and eggs, blending thoroughly.
4. Stir in rye flour.
5. Mix in foamy yeast.
6. Add whole wheat flour, 1 cup at a time, mixing well after each cup.
7. Mix in 1 cup all-purpose flour.
8. Knead last ¾ cup all-purpose flour into dough on table or board. Knead for 10 minutes until dough is smooth, firm and non-sticky.
9. Roll ball of dough in 1 teaspoon of the corn oil in bowl. Cover the bowl with clean towels and place in sink filled with a few inches of hot water. Let dough rise until double in bulk, about 2 hours.
10. Punch dough down and roll in the remaining 1 teaspoon corn oil in bowl. Cover and place in sink as before. Let rise for 1½ hours.

11. Divide dough in half and flatten each piece into a rectangular shape. Roll up length wise to form oblong loaves.

12. Sprinkle cornmeal on a buttered baking sheet. Roll the two loaves in the cornmeal until they are well covered. Place loaves on baking sheet far enough apart so that they will not touch when risen. Cover with paper towels and let rise until almost double in bulk, about 25 to 30 minutes.

13. Slash tops of risen loaves several times across their widths, about ½ inch deep.

14. Bake in preheated 375°F. oven for 45 to 50 minutes.

15. Cool on wire racks.

Health Breads

Health Bread

This is a nutritious whole wheat bread with bran, soy flour and wheat germ added. Make healthy sandwiches such as watercress and Bermuda onion. Then drink a glass of cold spring water and go climb a mountain!

1 serving hot cooked
   wheatena
1 cup milk
2 packages active dry
   yeast
3 tablespoons honey
1 cup lukewarm water
4 tablespoons plus
   2 teaspoons corn oil
2 tablespoons blackstrap
   molasses

2 teaspoons sea salt
2 eggs
2 tablespoons brewer's
   yeast
½ cup bran
½ cup soy flour
½ cup wheat germ
7½ cups stone-ground
   whole wheat flour
1 egg, slightly beaten
Poppy seeds

Yield: 3 loaves

1. Prepare wheatena as directed on box. (1 cup water, ¼ teaspoon salt and ¼ cup wheatena.) Put hot wheatena in a large mixing bowl.
2. Heat milk until lukewarm. Combine with wheatena.
3. Combine yeast, 1 tablespoon of the honey and water in a small bowl. Set aside in warm area until foamy and called for in recipe.

4. Add the 4 tablespoons corn oil, molasses, salt and the remaining 2 tablespoons honey to batter in large mixing bowl, blending thoroughly.

5. When batter has cooled to lukewarm, stir in 2 eggs.

6. Mix in brewer's yeast, bran, soy flour and wheat germ.

7. Add 1 cup whole wheat flour. Mix.

8. Stir in foamy yeast.

9. Add 5½ cups whole wheat flour, 1 cup at a time, mixing well after each cup.

10. Knead last 1 cup whole wheat flour into dough on table or board. Knead for about 10 minutes until dough is smooth and non-sticky.

11. Roll ball of dough in 1 teaspoon of the corn oil in bowl. Cover with clean towels and set in warm area to rise until double in bulk, about 1 hour.

12. Punch dough down and roll in the remaining 1 teaspoon corn oil in bowl. Cover with towels and let rise for 30 minutes.

13. Preheat oven at 375°F. Form three loaves and place in three buttered 9x5x3-inch loaf pans. Cover with a cloth and let rise until double in bulk, about 20 to 30 minutes.

14. Brush tops of risen loaves with beaten egg, and sprinkle poppy seeds on top. Bake for 40 to 50 minutes.

15. Cool on wire racks.

100% Whole Wheat Bread

This is a very high rising, hearty bread with a nice crust. It makes excellent sandwiches.

2 packages active dry
  yeast
5 tablespoons honey
½ cup lukewarm water
1 cup milk
¼ cup butter
2 teaspoons sea salt
3 tablespoons blackstrap
  molasses

1 tablespooon brewer's
  yeast
10½ cups stone-ground
  whole wheat flour
1 cup plain yogurt
4 eggs
2 teaspoons corn oil
1 egg, slightly beaten
Poppy seeds

Yield: 2 loaves

1. Combine yeast, 1 tablespoon of the honey and water in a small bowl. Set aside in warm area until foamy and called for in recipe.
2. Heat milk until hot, letting butter melt in it. Pour into a large mixing bowl.
3. Blend in the remaining 4 tablespoons honey, salt, molasses and brewer's yeast.
4. Add 2 cups flour, mixing well.
5. Mix in yogurt, then the eggs.
6. Add foamy yeast and stir.
7. Add 8 cups flour, 1 cup at a time, mixing well after each cup.
8. Knead last ½ cup flour into dough on table or board. Knead for 10 to 15 minutes until dough is smooth, elastic and non-sticky.
9. Roll ball of dough in 1 teaspoon of the corn oil in bowl. Cover bowl with a hot, damp towel and place it in the sink filled with a few inches of hot water. Let dough rise until double in bulk, about 1½ hours.
10. Punch dough down and roll in the remaining 1 teaspoon corn oil in bowl. Cover with a hot, damp towel and place in sink as before. Let dough rise for 1 hour.

11. Form two loaves and place in two buttered 9x5x3-inch loaf pans. Cover with a dry towel and let rise until double in bulk, about 45 to 50 minutes. Preheat oven at 375°F.

12. Brush beaten egg on top of risen loaves, and sprinkle poppy seeds on top.

13. Bake for 45 minutes.

14. Cool on wire racks.

Nutritious Whole Wheat Bread

A basic everyday bread that's nutritious and tasty.

2 servings cooked
  wheatena
2 packages active dry
  yeast
2 tablespoons honey
½ cup lukewarm water
1 cup plain yogurt
½ cup soy flour
½ cup wheat germ
2 teaspoons sea salt

2 tablespoons brewer's
  yeast
4 tablespoons plus
  2 teaspoons peanut oil
4 tablespoons blackstrap
  molasses
5 eggs
10½ cups stone-ground
  whole wheat flour
1 egg, slightly beaten

Yield: 2 loaves

 1. Prepare 2 servings wheatena as directed on package. Pour hot, cooked wheatena into a large mixing bowl.
 2. Combine yeast, honey and water in a small bowl. Set aside in warm area until foamy and called for in recipe.
 3. Stir yogurt into wheatena.
 4. Add soy flour and wheat germ, blending thoroughly.
 5. Mix in salt, brewer's yeast, the 4 tablespoons peanut oil and molasses.
 6. Add eggs and beat for a few minutes with a spoon.
 7. Blend in 2 cups whole wheat flour.
 8. Stir in foamy yeast.
 9. Add 8 cups whole wheat flour, 1 cup at a time, mixing well after each cup. Use your hands to mix in the last cup.
10. Knead final ½ cup whole wheat flour into dough on table or board. Knead for about 10 minutes until dough is smooth, soft and non-sticky.
11. Roll ball of dough in 1 teaspoon of the peanut oil in bowl. Cover with clean towels and place bowl in

sink filled with a few inches of hot water. Let dough rise for 1½ hours.

12. Punch dough down and roll in the remaining 1 teaspoon peanut oil in bowl. Cover with towels and place in sink as before. Let rise until double in bulk, about 1 hour.

13. Preheat oven at 375°F. Form two loaves and place in two buttered 9x5x3-inch loaf pans. Cover with a dry cloth and let rise until double in bulk, about 30 minutes.

14. Brush beaten egg on top of risen loaves.

15. Bake for 50 to 55 minutes.

16. Cool on wire racks.

Whole Wheat Molasses Oatmeal Bread

This is a very satisfying bread. It reminds me of a hot bowl of oatmeal with molasses on it on a cold, snowy winter morning. It has a hearty flavor and rises well.

2 packages active dry
   yeast
1 tablespoon honey
½ cup lukewarm water
1 cup boiling water
2 cups old-fashioned
   rolled oats
1 cup buttermilk
⅓ cup blackstrap
   molasses
2 teaspoons sea salt

3 tablespoons plus
   2 teaspoons corn oil
2 tablespoons brewer's
   yeast
½ cup wheat germ
½ cup soy flour
2 eggs
6¾ cups stone-ground
   whole wheat flour
1 egg, slightly beaten
   with 1 tablespoon milk

Rolled oats

Yield: 2 loaves

1. Combine yeast, honey and lukewarm water in a small bowl. Set aside in warm area until foamy and called for in recipe.
2. Pour boiling water into a large mixing bowl, then stir in rolled oats. Heat buttermilk until warm, not hot, and add to oats.
3. Stir in molasses, salt, the 3 tablespoons corn oil, brewer's yeast, wheat germ and soy flour, mixing thoroughly.
4. Beat in eggs.
5. Add 2 cups whole wheat flour. Mix well.
6. Mix in foamy yeast.
7. Add 4 cups whole wheat flour, 1 cup at a time. Mix well after each cup.
8. Knead last ¾ cup whole wheat flour into dough on table or board. Knead about 10 minutes until dough is smooth, firm and non-sticky.
9. Roll ball of dough in 1 teaspoon of the corn oil in bowl. Cover with a hot, damp towel and place in sink

filled with a few inches of hot water. Let dough rise for 1 hour.

10. Punch dough down and roll in the remaining 1 teaspoon corn oil in bowl. Cover with a hot, damp towel and place in sink as before. Let dough rise for 30 minutes.

11. Preheat oven at 375°F. Form two loaves and place in two buttered 9x5x3-inch loaf pans. Cover with a dry towel and let rise until double in bulk, about 25 minutes.

12. Brush tops of risen loaves with egg-milk mixture and sprinkle rolled oats on top.

13. Bake for 60 minutes.

14. Cool on wire racks.

Sunflower Yogurt Whole Wheat Bread

A very nutritious bread with lots of sunflower seeds. It's good with just butter and great with butter and jelly or with peanut butter and jelly.

2 packages active dry
  yeast
4 tablespoons honey
½ cup lukewarm water
1 cup milk
½ cup butter
1 cup plain yogurt
2 teaspoons sea salt
1 tablespoon brewer's
  yeast

½ cup wheat germ
3 eggs
8 cups stone-ground
  whole wheat flour
1 cup raw sunflower seeds
½ cup unbleached
  all-purpose flour
2 teaspoons corn oil
1 egg, slightly beaten
Sunflower seeds

Yield: 2 loaves

1. Combine yeast, 1 tablespoon of the honey and water in a small bowl. Set aside in a warm place until foamy and called for in recipe.
2. Heat milk until hot, letting butter melt in it. Pour into a large mixing bowl. Add yogurt and stir.
3. Add the 3 tablespoons honey, salt, brewer's yeast and wheat germ, blending thoroughly.
4. Beat in eggs.
5. Stir in 2 cups whole wheat flour.
6. Add foamy yeast, mixing.
7. Add 2 more cups whole wheat flour. Mix well.
8. Blend in sunflower seeds.
9. Add 4 cups whole wheat flour, 1 cup at a time, mixing well after each cup.
10. Knead all-purpose flour into dough on table or board. Knead for 5 to 10 minutes until dough is smooth, soft and non-sticky.
11. Roll ball of dough in 1 teaspoon of the corn oil in bowl. Cover with clean towels and let rise until double in bulk, about 2 hours.
12. Punch dough down and roll in the remaining 1 teaspoon corn oil in bowl. Cover and let rise for 1 hour.

13. Form two loaves and place in two buttered 9x5x3-inch loaf pans. Cover with a cloth and let rise until double in bulk, about 30 to 40 minutes. Preheat oven at 375°F.

14. Brush beaten egg on top of risen loaves and sprinkle raw sunflower seeds on top.

15. Bake for 40 minutes.

16. Cool on wire racks.

Bean Sprout Health Bread

This is a superb bread! It's both delicious and nutritious. High rising and light, the sunflower seeds and bean sprouts give it a nutty texture.

2 packages active dry
   yeast
¼ cup plus 1 tablespoon
   honey
½ cup lukewarm water
1 cup milk
¼ cup butter
1 cup creamed-style
   cottage cheese
2 teaspoons sea salt
2 tablespoons brewer's
   yeast
3 tablespoons blackstrap
   molasses

½ cup soy flour
½ cup wheat germ
½ cup cracked wheat
2 large eggs
8 cups stone-ground
   whole wheat flour
1 cup raw, unsalted
   sunflower seeds
2 cups coarsely chopped
   fresh bean sprouts
1 cup unbleached
   all-purpose flour
2 teaspoons corn oil
Melted butter

Yield: 2 loaves

1. Combine yeast, the 1 tablespoon honey and water in a small bowl. Set aside in a warm area until foamy and called for in recipe.
2. Heat milk until hot, letting butter melt in it. Pour into a large mixing bowl.
3. Blend in the ¼ cup honey, cottage cheese, salt, brewer's yeast and molasses.
4. Add soy flour, wheat germ and cracked wheat, mixing well.
5. Stir in eggs.
6. Add 2 cups whole wheat flour, blending thoroughly.
7. Mix in foamy yeast.
8. Stir in sunflower seeds.
9. Add bean sprouts to the batter.
10. Add 6 cups whole wheat flour, 1 cup at a time, mixing well after each cup.
11. Knead all-purpose flour into dough on table or

board. Knead vigorously for about 5 minutes until dough is firm, smooth and non-sticky.

12. Roll ball of dough in 1 teaspoon of the corn oil in bowl. Cover with a hot, damp towel and place bowl in sink filled with a few inches of hot water. Let dough rise until double in bulk, about 1 hour.

13. Punch dough down and roll in the remaining 1 teaspoon corn oil in bowl. Cover with a hot, damp towel and place in sink as before. Let rise for 30 minutes.

14. Preheat oven at 350°F. Form two loaves and place in two buttered 9x5x3-inch loaf pans. Cover with a dry towel and let rise in warm room until double in bulk, about 40 minutes.

15. Bake for 60 minutes.

16. Brush butter on tops.

17. Cool on wire racks.

Carrot Sunflower Seed Bread

This is a light, high-rising bread. Ricotta cheese makes it soft, sunflower seeds make it crunchy and carrots make it golden.

2 packages active dry
    yeast
¼ cup plus 1 tablespoon
    honey
½ cup lukewarm water
1 cup milk
½ cup butter
½ cup ricotta cheese
2 tablespoons brewer's
    yeast
2 teaspoons sea salt

3 eggs
5 cups stone-ground
    whole wheat flour
1 cup raw, unsalted
    sunflower seeds
2 cups grated carrots
4 cups unbleached
    all-purpose flour
2 teaspoons corn oil
1 egg, slightly beaten
Sunflower seeds

Yield: 2 loaves

1. Combine yeast, the 1 tablespoon honey and water in a small bowl. Set aside in warm area until foamy and called for in recipe.
2. Heat milk until hot, letting the butter melt in it. Pour into a large mixing bowl.
3. Stir in ricotta cheese, the ¼ cup honey, brewer's yeast and salt.
4. Add the eggs, beating for a minute or two with a spoon.
5. Blend in 2 cups whole wheat flour. Mix well.
6. Mix in foamy yeast.
7. Stir in sunflower seeds and carrots.
8. Add 3 cups whole wheat flour, 1 cup at a time, mixing well after each cup.
9. Add 3 cups all-purpose flour, 1 cup at a time, mixing well after each cup.
10. Knead last 1 cup of all-purpose flour into dough on table or board. Knead for 5 minutes until dough is smooth and non-sticky.

11. Roll ball of dough in 1 teaspoon of the corn oil in bowl. Cover bowl with a hot, damp towel and place in sink filled with a few inches of hot water. Let dough rise until double in bulk, about 1 hour.

12. Punch dough down and roll in the remaining 1 teaspoon corn oil in bowl. Cover and place in sink as before. Let dough rise for 30 minutes.

13. Preheat oven at 350°F. For two loaves and place in two buttered 9x5x3-inch loaf pans. Cover with a dry towel and let rise until double in bulk, about 30 minutes.

14. Brush beaten egg on top of risen loaves and sprinkle with raw sunflower seeds.

15. Bake for 60 minutes.

16. Cool on wire racks.

Bulgur Wheat Bread

The bulgur wheat gives this tasty bread a slightly crunchy texture.

2 servings cooked cream of wheat
2 packages active dry yeast
2 tablespoons honey
½ cup lukewarm water
½ cup sour cream
1½ teaspoons sea salt
3 tablespoons blackstrap molasses

1 cup bulgur
3 tablespoons plus 2 teaspoons corn oil
8 cups stone-ground whole wheat flour
3 eggs
1 cup unbleached all-purpose flour
1 egg, slightly beaten
Poppy seeds

Yield: 2 loaves

1. Prepare 2 servings cream of wheat: heat 2 cups milk until just boiling; add ½ teaspoon salt; stir in ⅓ cup of wheat; cook, stirring frequently, over medium heat until cereal is fairly thick. Pour into a large mixing bowl.
2. Combine yeast, honey and water in a small bowl. Set aside in warm area until foamy and called for in recipe.
3. Stir sour cream into cream of wheat.
4. Blend in salt, molasses, bulgur and the 3 tablespoons corn oil. Let cool to lukewarm.
5. Add 1 cup whole wheat flour. Mix.
6. Stir in eggs.
7. Mix in foamy yeast.
8. Add 7 cups whole wheat flour, 1 cup at a time, mixing well after each cup.
9. Knead all-purpose flour into dough on table or board. Knead for 5 to 10 minutes until dough is smooth and non-sticky.
10. Roll ball of dough in 1 teaspoon of the corn oil in bowl. Cover with clean towels. Let rise until double in bulk, about 1½ hours.

11. Punch dough down and roll in the remaining 1 teaspoon corn oil in bowl. Cover with towels and let rise for 1 hour.

12. Preheat oven at 375°F. Form two loaves and place in two buttered 9x5x3-inch loaf pans. Cover with a cloth and let rise until almost double in bulk, about 30 minutes.

13. Brush tops of risen loaves with beaten egg and sprinkle seeds on top.

14. Bake for 60 minutes.

15. Cool on wire racks.

Peanut Butter Peanut Bread

Kids love this nutty, wholesome, nutritious bread baked in a coffee can. It's great with butter and strawberry jam.

2 packages active dry yeast
¼ cup plus 1 tablespoon honey
½ cup lukewarm water
¼ cup butter
1 cup sour cream
½ cup peanut butter
2 teaspoons sea salt
1 cup wheat germ
2 eggs
2 cups stone-ground whole wheat flour
1 cup toasted, unsalted whole peanuts
2 cups plus 2 tablespoons unbleached all-purpose flour
Melted butter

Yield: 2 tall loaves baked in 1-pound coffee cans

1. Combine yeast, the 1 tablespoon honey and water in a small bowl. Set aside until foamy and called for in recipe.
2. Melt butter in a small pot, then add cream, stirring over low heat until hot. Pour into a large mixing bowl.
3. Add the ¼ cup honey, peanut butter and salt. Mix well, blending all ingredients.
4. Stir in wheat germ.
5. When batter is lukewarm, add eggs. Beat for a few minutes with spoon.
6. Mix in foamy yeast.
7. Thoroughly blend in whole wheat flour.
8. Stir in whole peanuts.
9. Add 2 cups all-purpose flour, mixing well. Knead last 2 tablespoons flour into dough on table or board. Knead for about 5 minutes.
10. Place in bowl and cover with clean towels. Let rise until double in bulk, about 2 or 3 hours.
11. Punch dough down. Let rise again until double in bulk, about 1 hour.

12. Divide dough in half and form two balls. Place in two well buttered 1-pound coffee cans. Press down. Cover with a cloth and let rise in warm area until dough is several inches above the top of the can, about 1 hour. Preheat oven at 350°F.

13. Bake for 35 minutes.

14. Tap coffee cans with spoon to loosen bread. Cool on wire racks. Brush tops with butter.

Bran Bread

Bran bread is easy to make and good to eat. It's dark, light textured and nutritious.

2 packages active dry
   yeast
3 tablespoons honey
½ cup lukewarm water
1 cup milk
½ cup butter
1 cup plain yogurt
2 teaspoons sea salt
2 tablespoons blackstrap
   molasses

2 cups 100% bran cereal
3 eggs
6 cups stone-ground
   whole wheat flour
2½ cups unbleached
   all-purpose flour
2 teaspoons corn oil
1 egg, slightly beaten
Poppy seeds

Yield: 2 loaves

1. Combine yeast, 1 tablespoon of the honey and water in a small bowl. Set aside in a warm area until foamy and called for in recipe.
2. Heat milk until hot, letting butter melt in it. Pour into a large mixing bowl.
3. Stir in yogurt.
4. Add the remaining 2 tablespoons honey, salt and molasses. Stir.
5. Blend in bran cereal.
6. Beat in eggs.
7. Add 2 cups whole wheat flour, mixing well.
8. Mix in foamy yeast.
9. Add 4 cups whole wheat flour, 1 cup at a time, mixing well after each cup.
10. Add 2 cups all-purpose flour, a little at a time, stirring well.
11. Knead last ½ cup all-purpose flour into dough on table or board. Knead for about 5 to 10 minutes until dough is soft, smooth and non-sticky.
12. Roll ball of dough in 1 teaspoon of the corn oil in bowl. Cover with clean towels and place bowl in sink filled with a few inches of hot water. Let dough rise for 1½ hours.

13. Punch dough down and roll in the remaining 1 teaspoon corn oil in bowl. Cover and place in sink as before. Let rise for 45 minutes.

14. Preheat oven at 375°F. Form two loaves and place in two buttered 9x5x3-inch loaf pans. Cover with a cloth and let rise in warm area until double in bulk, about 30 minutes.

15. Brush beaten egg on top of risen loaves and sprinkle poppy seeds on top.

16. Bake for 55 to 60 minutes.

17. Cool on wire racks.

Millet Bread

A nutritious, tasty bread with a slightly crunchy texture.

2½ cups hot cooked
   millet
2 packages active dry
   yeast
2 tablespoons honey
½ cup lukewarm water
1 cup sour cream
1 teaspoon sea salt
3 tablespoons plus
   2 teaspoons corn oil

2 eggs
2 heaping tablespoons
   brewer's yeast
1 cup wheat germ
4 cups stone-ground
   whole wheat flour
2½ cups unbleached
   all-purpose flour
1 egg, slightly beaten

Yield: 2 loaves

1. Prepare millet: bring 2 cups water to a boil in a small pot; add 1 teaspoon sea salt, 1 cup millet and 2 tablespoons butter; bring to a boil again; lower heat and simmer for 20 to 25 minutes; stir occasionally. Pour cooked millet into a large mixing bowl. Makes about 2½ cups cooked millet.
2. Combine yeast, honey and water in a small bowl. Set aside in a warm place until foamy and called for in recipe.
3. Stir sour cream, salt and the 3 tablespoons corn oil into millet.
4. Add eggs, blending thoroughly.
5. Blend in brewer's yeast and wheat germ.
6. Add foamy yeast, stirring.
7. Add whole wheat flour, 1 cup at a time, mixing well after each cup.
8. Add 2 cups all-purpose flour, a little at a time, mixing well.
9. Knead last ½ cup all-purpose flour into dough on table or board. Knead for 10 minutes until dough is smooth and non-sticky.

10. Roll ball of dough in 1 teaspoon of the corn oil in bowl. Cover with towels and place bowl in sink filled with a few inches of hot water. Let dough rise for 1½ hours.

11. Punch dough down and roll in the remaining 1 teaspoon corn oil in bowl. Cover with towels and let rise in sink as before for 1 hour.

12. Preheat oven at 375°F. Form two loaves and place in two buttered 9x5x3-inch loaf pans. Cover with a cloth and let rise until double in bulk, about 30 minutes.

13. Brush tops with beaten egg.

14. Bake for 50 to 55 minutes.

15. Cool on wire racks.

Anadama Health Bread

A superb bread! Delicious and nutritious, it is high-rising, soft and very dark. This loaf stays fresh and soft for a long time.

1 cup water
1 cup milk
2 teaspoons sea salt
½ cup undegerminated whole yellow cornmeal
⅓ cup butter
2 packages active dry yeast
1 tablespoon honey
½ cup lukewarm water
½ cup blackstrap molasses

½ cup wheat germ
2 tablespoons brewer's yeast
3 large eggs
½ cup soy flour
4 cups stone-ground whole wheat flour
2¾ cups unbleached all-purpose flour
2 teaspoons corn oil
Melted butter

Yield: 2 loaves

1. Prepare cornmeal mush: heat the 1 cup water and milk with ½ teaspoon of the salt in a pot over medium high heat until it comes to a boil. Slowly add cornmeal, stirring constantly so lumps don't form. Lower heat to medium. Add butter and stir until mush thickens. Pour into a large mixing bowl.

2. Combine yeast, honey and lukewarm water in a small bowl. Set aside in a warm area until foamy and called for in recipe.

3. Add the remaining 1½ teaspoons salt, molasses, wheat germ, and brewer's yeast to cornmeal mush, mixing well.

4. When batter is lukewarm stir in eggs, beating for a few minutes with a spoon.

5. Stir in soy flour.

6. Add 2 cups whole wheat flour, 1 cup at a time, mixing well after each cup.

7. Mix in foamy yeast.

8. Add 2 cups whole wheat flour, 1 cup at a time, mixing well after each cup.

9. Add 2 cups all-purpose flour, 1 cup at a time, mixing well.

10. Knead last ¾ cup all-purpose flour into dough on table or board. Knead for about 10 minutes until dough is smooth, soft and non-sticky.

11. Roll ball of dough in 1 teaspoon of the corn oil in bowl. Cover with clean towels and let rise for 2 hours.

12. Punch dough down and roll in the remaining 1 teaspoon corn oil in bowl. Cover with towels and let rise for about 1½ hours.

13. Form two loaves and place in two buttered 9x5x3-inch loaf pans. Cover with a cloth and let rise until double in bulk, about 45 minutes. Preheat oven at 375°F.

14. Bake for 40 minutes.

15. Brush butter on top of hot loaves.

16. Cool on wire racks.

Meat and Cheese Breads

Cheddar Cheese Wheat Sally Lunn

This spongy bread is especially good the next day when sliced, toasted in the oven and buttered.

2 packages active dry
  yeast
2 tablespoons honey
½ cup lukewarm water
1 cup milk
½ cup butter
2 teaspoons sea salt

2 cups stone-ground
  whole wheat flour
4 eggs
2 cups grated mild
  Cheddar cheese
2 cups unbleached
  all-purpose flour

Yield: 1 large loaf

1. Combine yeast, honey and water in a small bowl. Set aside in a warm place until foamy and called for in recipe.
2. Heat milk until hot, letting butter melt in it. Pour into a large mixing bowl.
3. Blend in salt and whole wheat flour.
4. Add eggs, beating with spoon for a few minutes.
5. Add cheese, mixing thoroughly.
6. Stir in foamy yeast.
7. Add all-purpose flour, beating for a few minutes with spoon.
8. Cover mixing bowl with an inverted bowl, and place in sink filled with a few inches of hot water. Let dough rise for 1 hour.

9. Stir dough down. Cover and place in sink as before. Let rise for 45 minutes.

10. Spoon batter into a well-buttered 10-inch tube pan. Cover and let rise until batter is about an inch from the top of the pan, about 1 hour.

11. Put bread in cold oven and set at 350°F. Bake for 60 minutes. Turn oven off. Open door and let bread sit in oven (with door open) for 10 minutes. A sudden change to cold air might make it fall.

12. Cool on a wire rack or serve hot.

Cheddar Wheat Bread

This is a soft, spongy bread with a crunchy crust and lots of flavor. It tastes even better after it's been frozen for a week so the flavors can mingle and settle. It tastes like spring.

2 packages active dry
  yeast
3 tablespoons honey
½ cup lukewarm water
¼ cup butter
⅔ cup cream cheese
½ cup sour cream
1 teaspoon sea salt
1 tablespoon dillweed
1 tablespoon chopped
  chives

¼ teaspoon chervil
¼ teaspoon summer
  savory
1¾ cups unbleached
  all-purpose flour
3 eggs
5 cups stone-ground
  whole wheat flour
2 cups grated Cheddar
  cheese
2 teaspoons corn oil

1 egg, slightly beaten

Yield: 2 loaves

1. Combine yeast, 1 tablespoon of the honey and water in a small bowl. Set aside in a warm area until foamy and called for in recipe.
2. Melt butter and cream cheese in a small pot over low heat. Add sour cream and cook, stirring, until mixture is lukewarm. Pour into a large mixing bowl.
3. Stir in the remaining 2 tablespoons honey, salt, dillweed, chives, chervil and summer savory.
4. Add 1 cup all-purpose flour, blending thoroughly.
5. Beat in eggs.
6. Mix in foamy yeast.
7. Blend in 2 cups whole wheat flour, mixing well.
8. Stir in cheese.
9. Add 3 cups whole wheat flour, 1 cup at a time, mixing well after each cup.
10. Knead last ¾ cup all-purpose flour into dough on table or board. Knead for 5 minutes until dough is soft and non-sticky.

11. Roll ball of dough in 1 teaspoon of the corn oil in bowl. Cover with towels and place bowl in sink filled with a few inches of hot water. Let dough rise until double in bulk, about 1 hour.

12. Punch dough down and roll in the remaining 1 teaspoon corn oil in bowl. Cover with towels and let rise in sink as before for 30 minutes.

13. Preheat oven at 350°F. Form two loaves and place in two buttered 9x5x3-inch loaf pans. Cover with a cloth and let rise until double in bulk, about 20 to 25 minutes.

14. Brush tops of risen loaves with beaten egg.

15. Bake for 50 minutes.

16. Cool on wire racks.

Ricotta Bread

This light, spongy bread rises very high; the loaves puff right out of the pans. The recipe was inspired by a delicious ricotta cookie my mother-in-law makes.

2 packages active dry
   yeast
7 tablespoons honey
1 cup lukewarm water
1 cup milk
½ cup butter
1 tablespoon sea salt

8 eggs
1 tablespoon vanilla
3 pounds ricotta cheese
17 cups unbleached
   all-purpose flour
4 teaspoons corn oil
1 egg, slightly beaten
Sesame seeds

Yield: 6 loaves

1. Combine yeast, 2 tablespoons of the honey and water in a small bowl. Set aside in a warm area until foamy and called for in recipe.

2. Heat milk until warm, letting butter melt in it. Pour into a large mixing pan (this is a big recipe so use a large pan instead of a bowl).

3. Stir in the remaining 5 tablespoons honey, salt, eggs and vanilla.

4. Heat ricotta cheese until warm. Add to batter, blending thoroughly.

5. Stir in 2 cups flour.

6. Mix in foamy yeast.

7. Add 13 cups flour, 1 cup at a time, mixing well after each cup.

8. Knead last 2 cups of flour into dough on table or board. Knead for about 10 minutes until dough is smooth, elastic and non-sticky.

9. Roll ball of dough in 2 teaspoons of the corn oil in pan. Cover with towels and let rise in warm room until double in bulk, about 1 hour.

10. Punch dough down and roll in the remaining 2 teaspoons corn oil in pan. Cover with towels and let rise for 30 minutes.

11. Preheat oven at 375°F. Divide dough in half. (Punch down one half, cover with towels and let rise until the first loaves are half baked.) Form three loaves with remaining half and place in three buttered 9x5x3-inch loaf pans. Cover with a cloth and let rise until double in bulk, about 20 minutes.

12. Brush beaten egg on top of risen loaves and sprinkle sesame seeds on top. Bake for 45 to 50 minutes. Cool on wire racks.

13. Form three loaves from the remaining dough when the first loaves are half baked. Let rise. Brush with egg. Bake.

Ricotta Wheat Bread

This bread makes the house smell so sweet when it's baking. It's a light wheat bread that is good for sandwiches.

2 packages active dry
  yeast
2 tablespoons honey
½ cup lukewarm water
½ cup butter
1 (15-ounce) container
  ricotta cheese
2 teaspoons sea salt

½ cup wheat germ
4 large eggs
2 teaspoons vanilla
4½ cups stone-ground
  whole wheat flour
2 cups unbleached
  all-purpose flour
2 teaspoons corn oil
Melted butter

Yield: 2 loaves

1. Combine yeast, honey and water in a small bowl. Set aside in a warm area until foamy and called for in recipe.
2. Melt butter in a small pot over low heat. Add ricotta cheese and cook, stirring, over medium heat until mixture is warm. Pour into a large mixing bowl.
3. Add salt, wheat germ and eggs, beating with a spoon for several minutes.
4. Blend in vanilla.
5. Add 1 cup whole wheat flour, mixing well.
6. Mix in foamy yeast.
7. Add 3½ cups whole wheat flour, a little at a time, mixing well as you add.
8. Stir in 1 cup all-purpose flour.
9. Knead last 1 cup all-purpose flour into dough on table or board. Knead for 5 to 10 minutes until dough is smooth, soft and non-sticky. (Do not add any more flour than necessary to make it non-sticky.)
10. Roll ball of dough in 1 teaspoon of the corn oil in bowl. Cover with clean towels and place bowl in sink filled with a few inches of hot water. Let dough rise until double in bulk, about 1 hour.

11. Punch dough down and roll in the remaining 1 teaspoon corn oil in bowl. Cover and place in sink as before. Let rise for 30 minutes.

12. Preheat oven at 350°F. Form two loaves and place in two buttered 9x5x3-inch loaf pans. Cover with a dry towel and let rise until double in bulk, about 20 to 25 minutes.

13. Bake for 50 to 55 minutes.

14. Brush butter on tops.

15. Cool on wire racks.

Blueberry-Cream Cheese Bread

What a light bread! And speckled with wild blueberries it's a real treat. My husband, Angelo, asked me to make a bread with blueberries and cream cheese in it. He thought it would be superb, and it is!

2 packages active dry
  yeast
½ cup plus 2 tablespoons
  honey
½ cup lukewarm water
2 cups milk
½ cup butter
1 (8-ounce) package
  cream cheese

16 cups unbleached
  all-purpose flour
1 tablespoon sea salt
4 eggs
1 (15-ounce) can wild
  Maine blueberries in
  heavy syrup
4 teaspoons corn oil
1 egg, slightly beaten
Poppy seeds

Yield: 4 loaves

1. Combine yeast, the 2 tablespoons honey and water in a small bowl. Set aside in a warm area until foamy and called for in recipe.
2. Heat milk until warm, letting butter melt in it. Add cream cheese and let partially melt. Pour into a large mixing pan and let cool to lukewarm (this is a big recipe so use a pan instead of a bowl).
3. Blend 1 cup flour in the cream cheese mixture.
4. Add salt, eggs and the ½ cup honey, stirring to blend.
5. Stir in blueberries with syrup.
6. Add 3 cups flour, 1 cup at a time, mixing well after each cup.
7. Mix in foamy yeast.
8. Add 10 cups flour, 1 cup at a time, mixing well after each cup.
9. Knead last 2 cups flour into dough on table or board. Knead for about 10 minutes until dough is smooth, elastic and non-sticky.
10. Roll ball of dough in 2 teaspoons of the corn oil in

pan. Cover with clean towels and let rise until double in bulk, about 1 hour.

11. Punch dough down and roll in the remaining 2 teaspoons corn oil in pan. Cover with towels and let rise for 30 minutes.

12. Preheat oven at 375°F. Form four loaves and place in four buttered 9x5x3-inch loaf pans. Cover with a cloth and let rise in a warm area until double in bulk, about 20 minutes.

13. Brush tops of risen loaves with beaten egg and sprinkle poppy seeds on top. Bake for 50 to 60 minutes.

14. Cool on wire racks.

Parmesan Garlic Bubble Loaf

A fancy, tasty bread that's perfect for serving with spaghetti. When you make Italian Sesame Seed Bread use half the dough for a sesame seed loaf and the other half for this bubble loaf.

Italian Sesame Seed dough (see recipe)
2 eggs, slightly beaten with 2 tablespoons cold water
1 cup grated Parmesan cheese
6 cloves garlic, slivered
Corn oil
1 teaspoon garlic powder
½ teaspoon sea salt

Yield: 1 bubble loaf

1. Prepare dough for Italian Sesame Seed Bread. Divide dough in half and use half for a seeded loaf and half for the bubble loaf.
2. To prepare the bubble loaf, cut about 22 to 25 small pieces of dough (each about the size of a large walnut) and roll each piece into a ball.
3. Roll each ball in the egg-water mixture then in grated Parmesan cheese.
4. Place the balls in a circular pattern in a buttered 10½-inch cast-iron frying pan. Leave a tiny bit of room between each ball for rising. Make one layer.

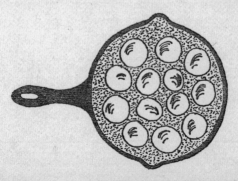

5. Sauté garlic in corn oil for a minute or so (if you sauté it for too long, it will burn in the oven). Sprinkle garlic over dough in pan.

6. Sprinkle garlic powder and salt over balls of dough.

7. Cover frying pan with a paper towel and let dough rise in a warm room for about 1 hour, or until double in bulk. Preheat oven at 400°F. Place a pan of hot water on bottom shelf of oven.

8. Bake at 400°F. for 5 minutes.

9. Lower heat to 350°F. and continue baking for 30 minutes.

10. Remove from frying pan and cool on a wire rack. Break apart to serve.

Bacon Potato Bread

This is a very light, high rising bread with a distinct bacon flavor, which comes out better the next day.

A. FIRST SPONGE:
2 packages active dry
  yeast
1 tablespoon honey
½ cup lukewarm water
1 cup mashed potatoes
2 cups potato water
2 teaspoons sea salt
3 cups unbleached
  all-purpose flour

B. REMAINING
  INGREDIENTS:
3 tablespoons honey
⅓ cup plus 3 teaspoons
  corn oil
4 large eggs
1 teaspoon sea salt
1 cup wheat germ
24 slices bacon
7½ cups unbleached
  all-purpose flour
Melted butter

Yield: 3 loaves

1. Combine yeast, 1 tablespoon honey and luke-warm water in a small bowl. Set aside in a warm area until foamy and called for in recipe.

2. Reserve 1 cup leftover mashed potatoes and 2 cups potato water (from boiling the potatoes) from a previous meal. When you're ready to make bread, reheat the potatoes in the potato water until hot. Pour into a large mixing pan. (My leftover mashed potaoes had milk and butter added, but no seasonings.)

3. Add 2 teaspoons salt and 3 cups flour, 1 cup at a time, to the potatoes, mixing well.

4. Blend in foamy yeast.

5. Beat the batter for a few minutes with a spoon. Cover pan with clean towels and set in sink filled with a few inches of hot water. (To prevent towels from sticking to dough, put an inverted pan over the mixing pan then hang towels over that.) Let sit for 4 to 5 hours. It will get bubbly.

6. After 4 to 5 hours beat dough down with spoon. Then add 3 tablespoons honey, the ⅓ cup corn oil, eggs, 1 teaspoon salt and wheat germ. Mix well.

7. Fry bacon until crisp, drain on paper towels and then crumble and add to batter, stirring to blend.

8. Add 7 cups flour, 1 cup at a time, mixing well after each cup.

9. Knead last ½ cup flour into dough on table or board. Knead for about 10 minutes until dough is light, spongy and non-sticky.

10. Roll ball of dough in 1 teaspoon of the corn oil in pan. Cover pan with clean towels and place in sink filled with a few inches of hot water. Let dough rise for 1½ hours.

11. Punch dough down and roll in 1 of the teaspoons corn oil in pan. Cover with towels and let rise for 45 minutes.

12. Punch dough down again and roll in the remaining 1 teaspoon corn oil. Cover pan and let dough rise for 30 minutes.

13. Preheat oven at 375°F. Form three loaves and place in three buttered 9x5x3-inch loaf pans. Cover with towels and let rise until double in bulk, about 30 minutes.

14. Bake for 55 to 60 minutes, or until golden brown.

15. Brush tops with butter.

16. Cool on wire racks.

Genoa Salami–Provolone Cheese Bread

Serve a thick slice of this bread with a fresh green salad and you've got a meal!

2 packages active dry
   yeast
1 tablespoon honey
½ cup lukewarm water
4 eggs
1 teaspoon sea salt
1 teaspoon black pepper

4 tablespoons plus
   2 teaspoons corn oil
2 cups chopped hard
   Provolone cheese
2 cups chopped Genoa
   salami (½ pound)
1 cup warm water

7 cups unbleached
   all-purpose flour

Yield: 2 loaves

1. Combine yeast, honey and lukewarm water in a small bowl. Set aside in a warm area until foamy and called for in recipe.
2. Put eggs, salt, pepper, the 4 tablespoons corn oil, cheese, salami and warm water in a large mixing bowl.
3. Stir in 2 cups flour.
4. Blend in foamy yeast.
5. Add 4 cups flour, 1 cup at a time, mixing well after each cup.
6. Knead last 1 cup of flour into dough on table or board. Knead for about 10 minutes until dough is smooth, elastic and non-sticky.
7. Roll ball of dough in 1 teaspoon of the corn oil in bowl. Cover with clean towels and let rise until double in bulk, about 1 hour.
8. Punch dough down and roll in the remaining 1 teaspoon corn oil in bowl. Cover with towels and let rise for 30 minutes.
9. Preheat oven at 375°F. Form two loaves and place in two buttered 9x5x3-inch loaf pans. Cover with a cloth and let rise for about 20 minutes, or until double in bulk.
10. Bake for 50 to 60 minutes.
11. Cool on wire racks.

Meat and Cheese Roll

Cut a thick slice of Meat and Cheese Roll, pour some hot cheese sauce over it, serve it with a fresh green salad and you have an entire meal. It's also very good as a leftover: slice it, toast it in the oven and pour hot cheese sauce over it.

DOUGH:
Challah recipe
Corn oil for pan

1 cup grated mellow
    Cheddar cheese
Grated Parmesan cheese

FILLING:
2 pounds ground round
    steak
1 medium-sized onion
2 cups fresh sliced
    mushrooms
2 tablespoons butter
1 teaspoon sea salt
¼ teaspoon pepper
1 teaspoon parsley flakes
1 teaspoon dried basil
    leaves
¼ pound pignolia nuts

TOPPING:
1 egg, slightly beaten
Poppy seeds
Pignolia nuts

SAUCE:
1 cup minced mushrooms
6 tablespoons butter
3 tablespoons all-purpose
    flour
2 cups milk
½ teaspoon salt
Pinch of pepper
2 cups grated mellow
    Cheddar cheese

Yield: 1 large Meat and Cheese Roll (12 to 14 slices)

1. Prepare Challah dough. After second rising divide dough in half. Using half the dough to form a loaf (as directed in Challah recipe) and the other half for this recipe.

2. Using fingertips and palms of hands, gently spread the dough on a large oiled baking sheet. Use oiled palms while spreading to ease out over the pan. Spread until dough is thin and covers surface of large rectangular baking sheet. (12″x18″)

3. Brown beef in frying pan, drain off grease and spread meat over dough.

4. Mince onion and sprinkle over meat.
5. Sauté sliced mushrooms in the butter, and sprinkle over meat.
6. Sprinkle salt, pepper, parsley flakes and basil on top.
7. Dot pignolia nuts over top here and there.
8. Spread Cheddar cheese on top.
9. Sprinkle Parmesan cheese over all.
10. Gently roll dough up lengthwise, pinch ends together and close all seams completely.
11. Cover with a towel and let rise until double in bulk, about 45 minutes. While roll rises preheat oven at 375°F.
12. Brush beaten egg on top of risen roll, and sprinkle poppy seeds on top. Sprinkle a few pignolia nuts here and there and press in lightly.
13. Bake for 45 minutes, or until golden brown.
14. Cool on wire rack for a few minutes.
15. Slice. Makes about 12 to 14 slices. Serve while still hot with cheese sauce.

Cheese Sauce

1. Sauté mushrooms in 2 tablespoons of the butter and set aside.
2. Melt the remaining 4 tablespoons butter in pot over medium heat.
3. Add flour, stirring until smooth.
4. Blend in milk and let simmer for 5 minutes.
5. Add salt and pepper.
6. Remove from heat. Add grated cheese, stirring until cheese melts. Stir in sautéed mushrooms.
7. Pour over hot slices of Meat and Cheese Roll.

Swiss Cheese and Onion Bread

This bread was inspired by quiche Lorraine. It's a light, high-rising, moist bread.

1 large onion, minced
2 packages active dry yeast
2 tablespoons honey
½ cup lukewarm water
½ cup plus 1 tablespoon butter
1 cup milk
2 teaspoons sea salt

1 cup wheat germ
2 cups stone-ground whole wheat flour
4 large eggs
2 cups grated Swiss cheese
4¼ cups unbleached all-purpose flour
2 teaspoons corn oil
1 egg, slightly beaten
Sesame seeds

Yield: 2 loaves

1. Sauté onion until golden in the 1 tablespoon butter in a small skillet and set aside.
2. Combine yeast, honey and water in a small bowl. Set aside in a warm place until foamy and called for in recipe.
3. Heat milk until hot, letting the ½ cup butter melt in it. Pour into a large mixing bowl.
4. Stir in salt and wheat germ.
5. When batter is lukewarm, mix in foamy yeast.
6. Add whole wheat flour, blending thoroughly.
7. Beat in eggs with a spoon.
8. Stir in sautéed onion and cheese.
9. Add 4 cups all-purpose flour, 1 cup at a time, mixing well after each cup.
10. Knead last ¼ cup all-purpose flour into dough on table or board. Knead for 5 to 10 minutes until dough is smooth and non-sticky.
11. Roll ball of dough in 1 teaspoon of the corn oil in bowl. Cover with clean towels and let rise for 2 hours.
12. Punch dough down and roll in the remaining 1 teaspoon corn oil in bowl. Cover with towels and let rise for 1 hour.

13. Preheat oven at 375°F. Form two loaves and place in two buttered 9x5x3-inch loaf pans. Cover with a towel and let rise until double in bulk, about 30 minutes.

14. Brush tops of risen loaves with beaten egg and sprinkle sesame seeds on top.

15. Bake for 30 minutes. Place a sheet of aluminum foil over tops of loaves to prevent burning. Continue baking another 10 to 15 minutes.

16. Cool on wire racks.

Sweet Breads

Hot Cross Buns

A light, sweet, spicy bread, that is good with hot cocoa or coffee.

2 packages active dry
    yeast
⅓ cup plus 1 tablespoon
    honey
½ cup lukewarm water
½ cup butter
1 cup plain yogurt
1 teaspoon sea salt
½ cup wheat germ
6 cups unbleached
    all-purpose flour

3 eggs
1 cup currants
Grated rind of 1 orange
1 teaspoon cinnamon
¼ teaspoon nutmeg
¼ teaspoon cloves
2 teaspoons corn oil
1 egg, slightly beaten
¾ cup confectioners'
    sugar
2 tablespoons orange juice

Yield: about 24 buns

1. Combine yeast, the 1 tablespoon honey and water in a small bowl. Set aside in a warm area until foamy and called for in recipe.
2. Melt butter in small pot over low heat. Add yogurt and cook, stirring, until warm. Pour into a large mixing bowl.
3. Blend in the ⅓ cup honey, salt and wheat germ.
4. Stir in 1 cup flour.
5. Add eggs, beating for a few minutes with a spoon.
6. Stir in 1 cup flour.
7. Add foamy yeast and mix.

8. Wash currants in warm water and drain. Add to batter, together with the orange rind, cinnamon, nutmeg and cloves.

9. Add 3 cups flour, 1 cup at a time, mixing well after each cup.

10. Knead last 1 cup flour into dough on table or board. Knead for 5 to 10 minutes until dough is smooth, soft and non-sticky.

11. Roll ball of dough in 1 teaspoon of the corn oil in bowl. Cover with clean towels and place bowl in sink filled with a few inches of hot water. Let dough rise until double in bulk, about 1½ hours.

12. Punch dough down and roll in the remaining 1 teaspoon corn oil in bowl. Cover and place in sink as before. Let rise for 45 minutes.

13. Preheat oven at 350°F. Cut off small pieces of dough about the size of a very large egg and place in buttered muffin tins. Cover with a clean cloth and let rise until double in bulk, about 30 minutes.

14. With sharp knife or razor slash tops of risen buns in crisscross formation, about ⅛ inch deep.

15. Brush tops with beaten egg.

16. Bake for 25 to 30 minutes.

17. Cool on wire racks.

18. Combine confectioners' sugar and orange juice. Fill crosses with frosting. If you want a thicker frosting use less juice.

19. Cool and let glaze harden.

Cardamom Christmas Buns

Here are some sweet breakfast buns that are light, fragrant and nutty.

2 packages active dry
  yeast
¼ cup plus 1 tablespoon
  honey
½ cup lukewarm water
1 cup plus 3 tablespoons
  milk
½ cup butter
2 teaspoons sea salt
6 cups unbleached
  all-purpose flour
2 eggs

1 teaspoon ground
  cardamom
1 teaspoon grated orange
  peel
1 cup finely ground
  slivered almonds
2 teaspoons corn oil
1 egg, slightly beaten with
  1 tablespoon milk
Slivered almonds
½ cup confectioners'
  sugar

2 teaspoons orange extract

Yield: 32 buns

1. Combine yeast, the 1 tablespoon honey and water in a small bowl. Set aside in a warm place until foamy and called for in recipe.
2. Heat 1 cup milk until hot, letting butter melt in it. Pour into a large mixing bowl. Stir in the ¼ cup honey.
3. Blend in salt and 2 cups flour.
4. Add eggs, beating for a few minutes with a spoon.
5. Mix in cardamom and orange peel.
6. Using a wooden rolling pin, grind 1 cup slivered almonds on a board then add to batter.
7. Add 3 cups flour, 1 cup at a time, mixing well after each cup.
8. Knead last 1 cup flour into dough on table or board. Knead for 5 to 10 minutes until dough is smooth, elastic and non-sticky.
9. Roll ball of dough in 1 teaspoon of the corn oil in bowl. Cover with clean towels and place bowl in sink filled with a few inches of hot water. Let dough rise for 1 hour.

10. Punch dough down and roll in the remaining 1 teaspoon corn oil in bowl. Cover with towels and let rise in sink as before for 45 minutes.

11. Punch dough down. Divide into four equal pieces and cut each fourth into eight equal pieces. Roll each piece with your hands to form balls. Place in buttered muffin tins and snip the top of each roll with scissors in a crisscross fashion. Cover with dry towels and let rise until double in bulk, about 30 minutes. While buns are rising preheat oven at 350°F.

12. Brush tops of risen buns with egg-milk mixture and sprinkle slivered almonds in center of each roll.

13. Bake for 20 to 25 minutes, or until golden brown.

14. Cool on wire racks.

15. Prepare glaze by combining confectioners' sugar, 3 tablespoons milk and orange extract, stirring until smooth. Brush tops of warm buns. Cool and let harden. (For a thicker glaze use less milk.)

Julebrød (Norwegian Christmas Bread)

This is my variation of Mom's *Julebrød*, which she made every Christmas. It's absolutely scrumptious! Butter a slice and eat it with a cup of hot cocoa or tea or coffee. What a treat!

CITRON:
Rind of 1 orange
Rind of 1 lemon
Fruit of ½ orange
Fruit of ½ lemon
1 cup boiling water
2 tablespoons honey

DOUGH:
2 packages active dry
  yeast
½ cup plus 1 teaspoon
  honey
½ cup lukewarm water
1 cup milk
½ cup butter
1 teaspoon sea salt
7 cups unbleached
  all-purpose flour

3 eggs
2 teaspoons ground
  cardamom
1 cup wheat germ
½ cup dark raisins,
  washed and drained
½ cup golden raisins,
  washed and drained
¼ cup currants, washed
  and drained
1 cup partially crushed
  walnuts
2 teaspoons corn oil
1 egg, slightly beaten

GLAZE:
1 cup confectioners' sugar
3 tablespoons milk
1 teaspoon vanilla

Yield: 2 round loaves

1. Prepare citron. For convenience, do this the day before you make the bread. Then refrigerate it and reheat it over low heat when ready to use it. It has to be warm when you put it in the batter.

Grate the orange and lemon rinds and put in a small pot. Cut up the orange and lemon into small pieces and add to the rind (be careful not to include pits). Add boiling water, cover and let come to a boil. Lower heat and cook, covered, for 1 hour. Most of the liquid will evaporate. Stir in honey. Cover and cook over low heat for 30 minutes longer, stirring occasionally. This makes about ½ cup citron. Cool to lukewarm, if using for the batter immediately.

2. Combine yeast, the 1 teaspoon honey and water in a small bowl. Set aside in warm place until foamy and called for in recipe.

3. Heat milk until hot, letting butter melt in it. Pour into a large mixing bowl.

4. Add the ½ cup honey and salt, stirring.

5. Add 1 cup flour, blending thoroughly.

6. Add eggs, beating for a few minutes with a spoon.

7. Stir in cardamom and wheat germ.

8. Mix in foamy yeast.

9. Add the lukewarm citron, raisins, currants and walnuts, mixing well.

10. Add 5 cups flour, 1 cup at a time, blending thoroughly after each cup.

11. Knead last 1 cup of flour into dough on table or board. Knead for about 5 minutes until dough is soft, smooth and only very slightly sticky.

12. Roll ball of dough in 1 teaspoon of the corn oil in bowl. Cover with a hot damp towel and place bowl in sink filled with a few inches of hot water. Let dough rise until double in bulk, about 1½ hours.

13. Punch dough down and roll in the remaining 1 teaspoon corn oil in bowl. Cover with a hot, damp towel and place in sink as before. Let rise for 30 minutes.

14. Punch dough down, and shape two round loaves. Place in two buttered 9-inch round cake pans with low rims. Cover with dry towel and let rise until almost double in bulk, about 30 to 40 minutes. Preheat oven at 350°F.

15. Brush beaten egg on top of risen loaves.

16. Bake for 50 to 60 minutes.

17. Cool on wire racks. Prepare glaze by combining confectioners' sugar, milk and vanilla. Brush on top of loaves and let harden.

18. Slice and butter.

Apple Gugelhupf

A superb, delicious, moist, mildly sweet coffee cake. It's perfect for breakfast or later in the day with coffee or tea. It lasts for a whole week when stored in a plastic bag in a bread box, but it's at its best the day after it's baked.

4 to 5 apples
1 package active dry yeast
½ cup plus 1 tablespoon honey
¼ cup lukewarm water
½ cup butter
1 cup plain yogurt
1 teaspoon sea salt
⅓ cup wheat germ
4 large eggs
4½ cups unbleached all-purpose flour

1 teaspoon vanilla
1 tablespoon grated lemon peel
1 tablespoon grated orange peel
½ cup dark raisins, washed and drained
½ cup currants, washed and drained
1 cup slivered almonds

Yield: 1 large coffee ring

1. Peel and chop into small pieces about 4 McIntosh, Cortland or other soft apples. Measure out 2 cups and set aside.
2. Combine yeast, the 1 tablespoon honey and water in a small bowl. Set aside in a warm place until foamy and called for in recipe.
3. Melt butter in a small pot. Add yogurt and cook, stirring, until warm. Pour into large mixing bowl.
4. With an electric mixer beat in the ½ cup honey, salt, wheat germ and eggs. Continue to beat for a few minutes.
5. Add 1 cup flour, beating for a few minutes with the electric mixer.
6. Add foamy yeast, mixing thoroughly.
7. Blend in vanilla and grated peels.
8. Stir in reserved apples, then raisins, currants and ½ cup of the almonds.

9. Add 3½ cups flour, 1 cup at a time, mixing well. Beat with spoon for 25 strokes or more. It will be a thick batter.

10. Cover bowl with dry towels and place in sink filled with a few inches of hot water. Let batter rise for 2 hours.

11. Beat batter down. Butter generously a 10-inch round tube pan. Sprinkle ¼ cup of the almonds on bottom and sides of pan. Nuts will stick to buttered surface.

12. Spoon the batter into the pan. Cover with a clean, dry cloth and set pan in warm area. Let batter rise until it's about 1 inch from the top of the pan, about 1¼ hours. Sprinkle the remaining ¼ cup almonds on top of risen batter. Preheat oven at 375°F. when batter is half risen.

13. Bake for about 45 minutes, or until golden brown, with the bread coming away from the sides of the pan. A toothpick will come out clean when inserted into the bread. (Do not overbake or it will dry out and the almonds will burn.)

14. Cool in pan for about 5 to 10 minutes, then carefully remove from pan. To remove center ring, place spatulas under bread and gently lift up as someone else slowly pushes down on the center ring until it's pushed out underneath the bread.

15. Cool on a wire rack.

16. Slice and eat as is or with butter.

Cinnamon Roll

This cinnamon roll is a beauty.

Sweet dough (recipe for
  Milk and Honey Bread)
¼ cup softened butter
½ cup dark brown sugar
3 tablespoons cinnamon
1 ounce poppy seeds
  (about half of a 2½-
  ounce box)

2 cups walnuts
½ cup dark raisins,
  washed and drained
1 egg, slightly beaten with
  2 tablespoons milk
1 cup confectioners' sugar
2 to 4 tablespoons milk
1 teaspoon vanilla

Yield: 1 large cinnamon roll

1. Prepare sweet dough. After it has risen twice, divide dough in half. Make 1 loaf (as directed in Milk and Honey Bread recipe), and use the remaining dough for the cinnamon roll.
2. Butter a dark 12x18-inch low-rimmed baking sheet. Use your hands to spread the dough gently out until it covers the surface of the pan. Use palms of hands and fingertips to spread the dough.
3. Spread softened butter over the dough.
4. Spread brown sugar on top of buttered dough.
5. Sprinkle cinnamon over sugar.
6. Sprinkle poppy seeds on top, then a layer of walnuts and finally the raisins.
7. Roll dough up lengthwise, sealing all edges well. Pinch seams together with fingertips.
8. Cover cinnamon roll with a cloth and let rise in warm room until double in bulk, about 40 minutes. Preheat oven at 350°F.
9. Brush top of risen roll with egg-milk mixture.
10. Bake for 25 to 30 minutes.
11. Cool on wire rack.
12. Frost when cool. Combine confectioners' sugar, milk and vanilla and spread over top of cinnamon roll. Slice and serve with butter.

Tapioca Walnut Bread

A moist, cake-like, mildly sweet breakfast bread that is chock full of nuts! This recipe makes two big, high-rising loaves.

2½ cups cooked tapioca
    pudding
2 packages active dry
    yeast
⅓ cup plus 1 tablespoon
    honey
½ cup lukewarm water
½ cup butter
3 eggs
¾ teaspoon sea salt

1 cup wheat germ
Grated rind of 1 orange
½ cup shredded coconut
3 cups stone-ground
    whole wheat flour
3 cups coarsely chopped
    walnuts
5 cups unbleached
    all-purpose flour
2 teaspoons corn oil

1 egg, slightly beaten

Yield: 2 loaves

1. Prepare "fluffy tapioca pudding" as directed on back of Minute Tapioca box (it makes about 2½ cups pudding). Pour into a large mixing bowl.
2. Combine yeast, the 1 tablespoon honey and water in a small bowl. Set aside in a warm area until foamy and called for in recipe.
3. Melt butter in small pot over low heat. Add to tapioca pudding.
4. Stir the ⅓ cup honey into mixture in bowl.
5. Blend in eggs, salt and wheat germ.
6. Stir in orange rind and coconut.
7. Add 1 cup whole wheat flour, blending thoroughly.
8. Mix in foamy yeast.
9. Add 2 cups whole wheat flour. Mix well.
10. Add walnuts.
11. Add 4 cups all-purpose flour, 1 cup at a time, mixing well after each cup. (You may have to use your hands to mix in the fourth cup.)
12. Knead last 1 cup of all-purpose flour into dough

on table or board. Knead for about 10 minutes until dough is smooth, soft and non-sticky.

13. Roll ball of dough in 1 teaspoon of the corn oil in bowl. Cover with clean towels and set bowl in sink filled with a few inches of hot water. Let rise until double in bulk, about 1½ hours.

14. Punch dough down and roll in the remaining 1 teaspoon corn oil in bowl. Cover with towels and let rise for 1 hour.

15. Form two loaves and place in two buttered 9x5x3-inch loaf pans. Cover with a clean cloth and let rise until almost double in bulk, about 40 to 45 minutes. Preheat oven at 375F°.

17. Brush tops of risen loaves with beaten egg.

18. Bake for 35 minutes. Put aluminum foil over tops of loaves and bake 10 minutes longer. The foil prevents the tops from getting too dark.

19. Cool on wire racks.

Concord Grape–Walnut Breakfast Bread

This breakfast bread is especially good when it's toasted and buttered. I bake it in September when the purple Concord grapes ripen in the vineyards of Marlboro, New York.

Concord grapes (5 to 6 small bunches) (1 cup cooked pulp)
¼ cup soft butter
1 package active dry yeast
1 cup plus 1 tablespoon raw sugar

½ cup lukewarm milk
1 teaspoon sea salt
2 eggs
1½ cups whole walnuts
5 cups unbleached all-purpose flour

Yield: 1 loaf and 6 muffins

1. Wash grapes and press each grape between your fingers to pop out the pulp into a small pot. Put the skins in a bowl.
2. Boil the pulp for a few minutes over low heat. Using a spoon, press the pulp through a sieve or colander into a bowl. Discard the seeds.
3. Combine the pulp and juice with the skins in a pot. Add butter and let it melt over low heat, stirring occasionally. Pour into a large mixing bowl and cool to lukewarm.
4. Combine yeast, the 1 tablespoon sugar and milk (which has been scalded and cooled). Set aside in a warm place until foamy and called for in recipe.
5. When grapes have cooled to lukewarm add the 1 cup sugar and salt, blending thoroughly.
6. Beat in eggs with a spoon.
7. Stir in walnuts.
8. Add 1 cup flour, mixing well.
9. Mix in foamy yeast.
10. Add 4 cups flour, 1 cup at a time, mixing well after each cup. Beat with a spoon for a few minutes.
11. Cover bowl with an inverted bowl or place and set in warm place to rise for 1½ hours.

12. Beat batter vigorously with a spoon. Spoon batter into a buttered 9x5x3-inch loaf pan and 6 sections of a buttered muffin tin. Cover with plates and let rise until double in bulk, about 1 hour and 45 minutes. Preheat oven at 350°F.

13. Bake 1 hour for the loaf and 30 minutes for the muffins.

14. Remove from pans. Cool on wire racks. Slice and butter.

Pumpkin Seed Pumpkin Bread

This is a moist, sweet, spicy bread that's delicious served for breakfast.

1 package active dry yeast
1 cup plus 1 tablespoon
  sugar
½ cup lukewarm milk
1 cup warm, cooked
  pumpkin
2 eggs
1 teaspoon sea salt
¼ cup butter

1 teaspoon cinnamon
½ teaspoon nutmeg
1 cup shelled unsalted
  pumpkin seeds
1 cup stone-ground
  whole wheat flour
2 cups unbleached
  all-purpose flour

Yield: 1 loaf

1. Combine yeast, the 1 tablespoon sugar and milk (which has been scalded and cooled) in a small bowl. Set aside in a warm area until foamy and called for in recipe.
2. Cook pumpkin, eggs, salt and butter in a pot over medium heat until butter melts and mixture is warm. Pour into a large mixing bowl.
3. Blend in the 1 cup sugar, cinnamon and nutmeg, stirring until smooth.
4. Add pumpkin seeds.
5. Stir in whole wheat flour.
6. Mix in foamy yeast.
7. Add all-purpose flour, beating vigorously with a spoon.
8. Cover bowl with a dish and let rise in warm area for 1 hour and 15 minutes.
9. Beat batter vigorously for a few minutes. Spoon batter into a buttered 9x5x3-inch loaf pan. Cover with plate, and let rise for about 45 minutes, or until it rises to just below the rim of the pan.
10. Preheat oven at 350°F. Bake for 1 hour and 10 minutes.
11. Remove from pan. Cool on wire rack. Slice and butter.

Portuguese Sweet Bread

My husband loves this bread. It's a light, round, mildly sweet loaf.

2 packages active dry
  yeast
½ cup plus 1 tablespoon
  honey
¼ cup lukewarm water
¾ cup milk
½ cup butter

2 teaspoons sea salt
6 cups unbleached
  all-purpose flour
3 large eggs
½ cup wheat germ
2 teaspoons corn oil
1 egg, slightly beaten

Yield: 2 round loaves

1. Combine yeast, the 1 tablespoon honey and water in a small bowl. Set aside in a warm area until foamy and called for in recipe.
2. Heat milk until hot, letting butter melt in it. Pour into a large mixing bowl.
3. Stir in the ½ cup honey and salt.
4. Add 2 cups flour, blending thoroughly.
5. Add eggs, beat with a spoon for a few minutes, then blend in wheat germ.
6. Add foamy yeast and mix well.
7. Add 3 cups flour, 1 cup at a time, mixing well after each cup.
8. Knead last 1 cup flour into dough on table or board. Knead for about 10 minutes until dough is smooth, soft and non-sticky.
9. Roll ball of dough in 1 teaspoon of the corn oil in bowl. Cover with clean towels and place bowl in sink filled with a few inches of hot water. Let dough rise for 2 hours.
10. Punch dough down and roll in the remaining 1 teaspoon corn oil in bowl. Cover and let rise in sink as before for 2 hours.
11. Form two round loaves and place in two buttered 9-inch round cake pans with low sides. Cover with a cloth and let rise until double in bulk, about 1 hour.

12. Preheat oven at 350°F. Bake for 30 minutes. Cover top of loaves loosely with aluminum foil so they won't get too dark. Bake 15 minutes longer. Remove loaves from cake pans and place on a flat, rimless baking sheet. Bake for 5 to 10 minutes longer with aluminum foil over tops. Total baking time is 50 to 55 minutes.
13. Cool on wire racks.

Apple-Date-Nut Loaf

A soft, sweet, moist breakfast or tea bread with a great flavor.

1 package active dry yeast
¼ cup plus 1 tablespoon honey
½ cup lukewarm water
½ cup plain yogurt
¼ cup butter
2 cups stone-ground whole wheat flour
2 eggs
1 teaspoon sea salt

2 large apples (1½ cups finely chopped)
½ cup chopped dates
1 cup coarsely chopped pecans
½ teaspoon cinnamon
3½ cups unbleached all-purpose flour
2 teaspoons corn oil
1 egg, slightly beaten

Yield: 2 loaves

1. Combine yeast, the 1 tablespoon honey and water in a small bowl. Set aside in a warm place until foamy and called for in recipe.
2. Heat yogurt and butter in a small pot until butter melts and liquid is warm. Pour into a large mixing bowl.
3. Stir in the ¼ cup honey.
4. Add 1 cup whole wheat flour, blending thoroughly.
5. Mix in foamy yeast.
6. Add 1 cup whole wheat flour. Mix well.
7. Beat in eggs with a spoon.
8. Add salt.
9. Peel and finely chop 2 large apples to measure 1½ cups. Stir into batter.
10. Stir in dates.
11. Blend in pecans and cinnamon.
12. Add 3 cups all-purpose flour, 1 cup at a time, mixing well after each cup.
13. Knead last ½ cup flour into dough on table or board. Knead for about 5 minutes to form a soft, nonsticky dough.

14. Roll ball of dough in 1 teaspoon of the corn oil in bowl. Cover with clean towels and let rise for 2 hours.
15. Punch dough down and roll in the remaining 1 teaspoon corn oil in bowl. Cover with towels and let rise for 1 hour.
16. Form 2 loaves and place in two buttered 8½ x 5½ x 3⅝-inch loaf pans. Cover with a cloth and let rise until double in bulk, about 1 hour. Preheat oven at 350°F.
17. Brush tops of risen loaves with beaten egg.
18. Bake for 35 to 45 minutes.
19. Cool on wire racks.

Mother's Day Coffee Roll and Sour Cream Loaf

This recipe makes three filled coffee rolls shaped into the letters MOM for Mother's Day, one regular coffee roll, and one loaf of soft, very high-rising bread. The delicious filling in the rolls is a combination of ricotta cheese, chocolate chips, nuts and dates with other good things.

DOUGH:
2 packages active dry yeast
¼ cup plus 1 tablespoon honey
½ cup lukewarm water
1 cup sour cream
½ cup milk
1 cup butter
2 teaspoons sea salt
9 cups unbleached all-purpose flour
3 whole eggs plus 3 egg yolks
2 teaspoons corn oil
1 egg, slightly beaten
Sesame seeds

FILLING:
½ cup melted butter
½ cup honey
1 cup ricotta cheese
2 eggs
1 teaspoon vanilla
1 tablespoon grated lemon rind
1 cup wheat germ
1 cup chopped dates
2 cups coarsely chopped walnuts
1 (6-ounce) package chocolate chips

GLAZE:
2 to 3 tablespoons milk
1 cup confectioners' sugar
Decorator candies

Yield: 3 filled rolls in shape of MOM
1 regular filled roll
1 loaf of bread

1. For the dough, combine yeast, 1 tablespoon honey and water in a small bowl. Set aside in a warm place until foamy and called for in recipe.
2. Cook sour cream, milk and butter in a small pot over low heat until butter melts and liquid is very warm. Pour into a large mixing bowl.
3. Stir in the ¼ cup honey and salt.
4. Blend in 2 cups flour.

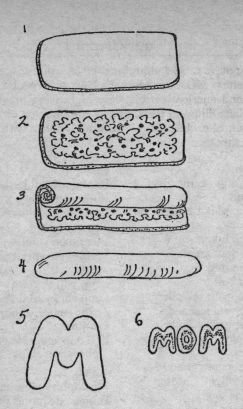

5. Add eggs and egg yolks, mixing well.

6. Mix in foamy yeast.

7. Add 6 cups flour, 1 cup at a time, mixing well after each cup.

8. Knead last 1 cup flour into dough on table or board. Knead 5 to 10 minutes. This is a soft, easy to work with dough.

9. Roll ball of dough in 1 teaspoon of the corn oil in bowl. Cover with clean towels and let rise for 1 hour.

10. Punch dough down and roll in the remaining 1 teaspoon corn oil in bowl. Cover bowl loosely with plastic wrap and refrigerate for at least 3 hours.

11. Remove from refrigerator and let dough rise for 30 minutes at room temperature.

12. Preheat oven at 350°F. Prepare the filling by combining the melted butter, honey, ricotta, eggs, vanilla and lemon rind. Blend in wheat germ, dates and walnuts. Stir in chocolate chips. Set filling aside.

13. Cut off a piece of dough about the size of a man's first. Roll it out on an unfloured board into a thin rectangular shape about 12 inches long, 6 inches wide and ⅛ inch thick. Put about 2 to 3 tablespoons of filling along the middle length of the dough. Fold over one flap of dough, then fold over remaining flap. Pinch all seams and the ends together tightly. Place on buttered baking sheet. Shape it into the letter M. Form another filled M and place on same baking sheet. Make sure all seams are closed tightly. Cover with a cloth and let rise for 20 to 30 minutes. Brush beaten egg on top. Bake for 30 minutes, or until golden brown. Cool on wire racks.

14. While the two M's are baking, shape the filled O by pinching the two ends of a filled roll together in a circle. Let rise, brush with egg and bake for 30 minutes. Cool on wire rack.

15. While the O bakes, shape a regular filled roll (as for a cinnamon roll) with half of the remaining dough. Use the rest of the filling in this. Let rise, brush with egg and bake until golden brown.

16. Shape a loaf with the remaining dough. Place it in a buttered 8½x5½x3⅝-inch loaf pan. Let rise until double in bulk. Brush with egg and sprinkle sesame seeds on top. Bake at 350°F. for 40 minutes. This loaf puffs up very high.

17. When the MOM filled rolls have partially cooled, prepare the glaze. Blend milk and confectioners' sugar thoroughly. Drop the glaze by teaspoon on the rolls, clarifying the shape of the letters MOM even more. Then add the decorator candies in a way that makes the letters MOM even more distinct.

18. Cool thoroughly. Give it to Mom.

Barmbrack

The Irish serve this sweet bread on Halloween. They sometimes put a wedding ring in the bread and the finder will supposedly find love within that year. This is my version of it, adding wheat germ and using honey rather than sugar. It's a soft, sweet breakfast bread.

1 package active dry yeast
½ cup plus 1 tablespoon honey
¼ cup lukewarm water
1 cup milk
½ cup butter
7¼ cups unbleached all-purpose flour
1 teaspoon sea salt

4 eggs
1 cup wheat germ
1 teaspoon allspice
Grated rind of 1 orange
2 cups currants, washed and drained
2 teaspoons corn oil
Butter for tops
Sugar for tops

Yield: 2 round loaves

1. Combine yeast, the 1 tablespoon honey and water in a small bowl. Set aside in a warm place until foamy and called for in recipe.
2. Heat milk until hot, letting butter melt in it. Pour into a large mixing bowl.
3. Stir in the ½ cup honey and salt.
4. Blend in 2 cups flour.
5. Beat eggs in with a spoon.
6. Mix in wheat germ.
7. Add foamy yeast.
8. Stir in allspice and orange rind.
9. Mix in currants.
10. Add 5 cups flour, 1 cup at a time, mixing well after each cup.
11. Knead last ¼ cup flour into dough on table or board. Knead 5 to 10 minutes to form a firm, non-sticky dough. (These are free standing loaves.)
12. Roll ball of dough in 1 teaspoon of the corn oil in bowl. Cover with clean towels and let rise in warm room for 2 hours.

13. Punch dough down and roll in the remaining 1 teaspoon corn oil in bowl. Cover with towels and let rise for 1½ hours.

14. Form two round loaves and place in two buttered 9-inch round cake pans with low rims. Cover with a cloth and let rise until double in bulk, about 1 hour. Preheat oven at 350°F.

15. Bake for 25 minutes. Remove from cake pans and bake another 25 to 30 minutes on a flat baking sheet. Put aluminum foil over tops to prevent them from getting too dark.

16. Cool on wire racks. Brush tops of hot loaves with butter and sprinkle with sugar.

Sourdough Breads

Long Sourdough French Loaves

This bread has a wonderful crust.

STARTER:
1 package active dry yeast
1 tablespoon honey
2 cups warm water
3 cups unbleached all-purpose flour

Use a wooden spoon to mix the above ingredients in an earthenware bowl. (Do not use metal with sourdough.) Beat for a few minutes with the spoon. Cover bowl loosely with paper towels and leave in a warm room for two or three days. Stir down daily, using the wooden spoon. Refrigerate in covered crock. Stir daily.

To REPLENISH STARTER after using 1 cup of it for this French Bread recipe (or any recipe), add 1 cup flour and 1 cup warm water. Beat for a few minutes with a wooden spoon. Cover loosely and leave in warm room for a day or two. Stir daily.

If you don't use it within a few days store the starter in a tightly covered glass jar or earthenware crock in the refrigerator. (Do not use metal top. I put plastic wrap on top of my starter crock and secure it with an elastic band.) Use a jar or crock that's big enough to allow starter room to rise, or fill the jar only halfway. Stir down daily. If you don't use any sourdough within a week, remove and discard a cup of it and replenish as directed above.

When using starter that has been refrigerated, take it out several hours before making bread so that it can return to room temperature.

DOUGH:
1 cup sourdough starter
1 package active dry yeast
1 tablespoon honey
½ cup lukewarm water
1 cup warm water
1 cup warm milk
2 teaspoons sea salt

3 tablespoons plus
   2 teaspoons corn oil
1 cup wheat germ
6½ cups unbleached
   all-purpose flour
Cornmeal for pan
1 egg white mixed with
   1 tablespoon water

Salt water (½ teaspoon
   salt dissolved in ½ cup
   water)

Yield: 2 long loaves

1. Prepare sourdough starter as directed above several days ahead of time, or if you have some old starter in the refrigerator take it out several hours before preparing dough so that it can warm up to room temperature.

2. Combine yeast, honey and lukewarm water in a small bowl. Set aside in a warm place until foamy and called for in recipe.

3. Put warm water and milk in a large mixing bowl. Stir in salt, the 3 tablespoons corn oil, wheat germ and starter.

4. Blend in 2 cups flour.

5. Add foamy yeast. Mix.

6. Mix in 1 cup flour. Cover bowl with plate and set it in a warm area for 2 hours to let dough rise and sour.

7. Stir batter down after 2 hours. Add 3 cups flour, 1 cup at a time, mixing well after each cup.

8. Knead last ½ cup flour into dough on table or board. Knead for 10 minutes until dough is smooth, firm and non-sticky.

9. Roll ball of dough in 1 teaspoon of the corn oil in bowl. Cover with clean towels and let rise until double in bulk, about 1½ hours.

10. Punch dough down and roll in the remaining 1 teaspoon corn oil in bowl. Cover and let rise for 1 hour.

11. Place a pan of hot water on the bottom shelf of the oven. Divide dough in half. Punch down one-half, cover and set aside. Take remaining half and use your hands to flatten it out on the table into a long rectangular shape. Roll dough up lengthwise into a long, thin loaf. Pinch seams and taper ends. Place loaf, seam side down, on a buttered baking sheet that has had cornmeal sprinkled on it. Cover with a dry cloth and let rise until double in bulk, about 30 minutes. Preheat oven at 400°F.

12. With a sharp knife slash top of risen loaf 3 or 4 times across the width, about ¼ inch deep.

13. Brush egg white-water mixture on top of slashed loaf.

14. Bake at 400°F. for 15 minutes.

15. Remove pan of water and reduce heat to 350°F. Brush loaf with salt water. Bake 15 minutes longer.

16. Now you can shape the second loaf, cover and let rise.

17. Brush first loaf once more with salt water. Bake a final 15 to 20 minutes, or until golden brown and hollow sounding when tapped underneath loaf. Total baking time is 45 to 50 minutes.

18. Cool on wire rack with cold air from fan blowing on loaf to crackle crust.

19. Store completely cooled bread in brown bag in refrigerator. Do not store in bread box or crust will soften.

Note: When first loaf is a little more than half done, prepare the second loaf and let it rise. Bake as directed. Or if you're lucky enough to own French bread forms you can bake both loaves at the same time.

Sourdough Hard Rolls

You can make big rolls for hero sandwiches or small ones to serve with dinner. These have a nice crisp crust.

1 cup sourdough starter
3 packages active dry yeast
1 tablespoon light molasses
1 cup lukewarm water
1 cup warm water
2 teaspoons sea salt
1 cup semolina flour
⅔ cup wheat germ

4¾ to 5 cups unbleached all-purpose flour
2 tablespoons corn oil
Cornmeal for pan
1 egg white mixed with 1 tablespoon water
Sesame seeds
Salt water (½ teaspoon salt dissolved in ½ cup water)

Yield: 12 large rolls or 16 small rolls or a combination

1. Prepare sourdough starter a few days before preparing bread (if you haven't any handy). See Sourdough French Bread recipe for starter recipe.
2. Combine yeast, molasses and lukewarm water in a small bowl. Set aside in a warm place until foamy and called for in recipe.
3. Pour warm water into a large mixing bowl. Mix in salt and semolina flour.
4. Beat in starter with a wooden spoon.
5. Mix in wheat germ and foamy yeast.
6. Add 4 cups flour, 1 cup at a time, mixing well after each cup.
7. Knead last ¾ to 1 cup flour into dough on table or board. Knead vigorously for 20 to 25 minutes until dough is firm, smooth and non-sticky. (It is important to knead this bread long and well.)
8. Roll ball of dough in 1 tablespoon of the corn oil in bowl. Cover with clean towels and let rise for 1 hour, or until double in bulk.
9. Punch dough down and roll in the remaining 1 tablespoon corn oil in bowl. Cover with towels and let rise for 45 minutes.

10.   Divide dough into 12 or 16 pieces. Use your hands to flatten each piece into a rectangular shape on the table. Then roll up to form a long roll and taper ends. Place on large baking sheets that have been buttered and then sprinkled with cornmeal. Cover with a clean cloth and let rise until double in bulk, about 20 to 30 minutes.

11.   Using a sharp knife or razor slash risen rolls twice across the width, about ¼ inch deep.

12.   Brush egg white-water mixture on top of slashed rolls and sprinkle sesame seeds on top.

13.   Bake in preheated over at 375°F. for about 10 minutes.

14.   Brush salt water on rolls and bake another 10 minutes.

15.   Brush salt water on rolls and bake a final 10 minutes, if rolls are small. (Add an extra 5 to 10 minutes baking time for large rolls.) Rolls will be golden brown and sound hollow when tapped if done. Total baking time is about 30 to 40 minutes, depending on size of rolls.

16.   Cool on wire racks with cold air from fan blowing on rolls to crackle crust.

17.   Store in brown bag in refrigerator. Freeze some. But do not store in bread box or crust will soften.

Sourdough Onion Rye Bread

This recipe makes four small loaves of tasty sourdough rye with a very flavorful topping of sour cream and onion.

STARTER:
2 cups lukewarm water
2 cups unbleached
  all-purpose flour
1 tablespoon honey
1 package active dry yeast

BEGIN DOUGH ONE EVENING:
1 cup hot milk
4 tablespoons honey
1 cup sourdough starter
1½ cups stone-ground
  rye flour
1½ cups unbleached
  all-purpose flour

CONTINUE NEXT MORNING:
1 package active dry yeast

1 tablespoon honey
¼ cup lukewarm water
2 teaspoons sea salt
3 tablespoons melted
  butter
½ cup rye flour
3 cups unbleached
  all-purpose flour
2 teaspoons corn oil

TOPPING:
1 egg, slightly beaten
½ cup sour cream
1 teaspoon onion powder
½ cup minced onion
1 tablespoon butter
4 teaspoons kosher salt

Yield: 4 small loaves

1. *Prepare starter* two or three days ahead of time. Combine water, flour, honey and yeast in a large earthenware bowl. Use a wooden spoon (do not use metal with sourdough). Cover bowl loosely with paper towels and let stand in a warm room for two or three days. Stir down daily. (See Sourdough French Bread recipe for further information.)

2. After the starter has soured sufficiently *begin the dough one evening.* Pour milk into a large earthenware mixing bowl. Add honey and stir. Cool to lukewarm. Blend in starter and flours. Mix well. Cover loosely with paper towels and leave in a warm room overnight. (Be sure to use a very large bowl for the dough rises very high.)

3. *Continue the next morning.* Combine yeast, honey and water in a small bowl. Set aside until foamy.

Stir down the dough in the large mixing bowl. Add salt, butter and rye flour. Mix well, then stir in foamy yeast.

Add 2 cups all-purpose flour, 1 cup at a time, mixing well after each cup. Knead last 1 cup all-purpose flour into dough on table or board. Knead for about 10 minutes until dough is smooth and non-sticky.

Roll ball of dough in 1 teaspoon of the corn oil in bowl. Cover with towels and let rise until double in bulk, about 2 hours. Punch dough down and roll in the remaining 1 teaspoon corn oil in bowl. Cover with towels and let rise for 1½ hours.

4. *Shape* four small round loaves and place on a large buttered baking sheet. Cover loaves with a cloth and let rise until double in bulk, about 40 minutes. Preheat oven at 375°F.

5. *Preparing topping.* Mix together egg, sour cream and onion powder. Sauté minced onion in butter until onion is golden. Stir into sour cream mixture.

Using a sharp knife or razor slash risen loaves in crosscross fashion, about ¼ inch deep. Gently spread the sour cream mixture on top of the loaves. Sprinkle 1 teaspoon kosher salt on top of each loaf.

6. Bake for 40 to 45 minutes. Cool on wire racks.

Note: Store the remaining starter in crock or glass jar in refrigerator; do not use a metal top.

Sourdough Super Crusty Rye in Cast-Iron Pan

Crust lovers will love this sourdough rye. Baking it in a cast-iron frying pan gives it a wonderful crust.

DO IN AFTERNOON:

1 cup sourdough starter
1 cup warm water
1 cup stone-ground rye flour
1 cup unbleached all-purpose flour

DO NEXT MORNING:

1 package active dry yeast
2 tablespoons honey
½ cup lukewarm water
½ cup hot water
3 tablespoons plus 2 teaspoons corn oil

2 teaspoons sea salt
½ cup wheat germ
1 cup stone-ground rye flour
3½ cups unbleached all-purpose flour
1 egg white mixed with 1 tablespoon water
Cornmeal for pan
Salt water (1 teaspoon salt dissolved in ½ cup water)

Yield: 2 loaves

1. If you haven't any handy, prepare starter at least three days in advance to allow time for it to sour properly (see instructions for starter in Sourdough French Bread recipe).

2. *One afternoon* when the starter is ready to use (and is at room temperature if it's old starter from the refrigerator), combine 1 cup of starter with water and flours. Use an earthenware bowl and a wooden spoon. Use a very large bowl for the dough will rise very high overnight. Cover the bowl loosely with plastic wrap. Stir it down before going to bed. Let it sit overnight in a warm room.

3. *The next morning* combine yeast, honey and lukewarm water in a small bowl. Set aside in a warm place until foamy and called for in recipe.

Stir down the dough that was prepared the previous afternoon in the large mixing bowl. Add hot water and mix well. Blend in the 3 tablespoons corn oil, salt and wheat germ. Mix in foamy yeast and rye flour.

Add 2½ cups all-purpose flour, a little at a time, mixing well as you add. Knead last 1 cup all-purpose flour into dough on table or board. Knead for 15 to 20 minutes until dough is firm, smooth and non-sticky.

Roll ball of dough in 1 teaspoon of the corn oil in bowl. Cover with a hot, damp towel and place bowl in sink filled with a few inches of hot water. Let dough rise until double in bulk, about 1 hour. Punch dough down and roll in the remaining 1 teaspoon corn oil in bowl. Cover and place in sink as before. Let rise for 30 minutes.

4. *Shape* dough into two round loaves and place them in buttered, cornmeal sprinkled 10½-inch cast-iron frying pans. Cover with dry towels and let rise until double in bulk, about 20 to 25 minutes. Preheat oven at 400°F. Place a pan of hot water on bottom shelf of oven to create steam for a good crust.

With a sharp knife or razor, slash tops of risen loaves about ¼ inch deep, but not deeper. Make two parallel slashes. Brush egg white-water mixture on top.

5. *Bake* at 400°F. for 15 minutes. Remove pan of water and reduce heat to 350°F. Brush loaves with salt water. Bake for 30 minutes. Remove loaves from frying pans and place on a large baking sheet. Brush again with salt water. Bake a final 15 to 20 minutes. Total baking time is about 60 to 65 minutes. Bread is placed on baking sheet for final baking so that the rough lower crust can get fully baked; the sides of the frying pan create the crusty roughness but prevent it from baking thoroughly on the lower one-third.

6. Cool on wire racks with cold air from fan blowing on bread to crackle crust. Do not store in bread box or crust will soften.

Special Breads

Sour Cream Onion Rolls

These are very light, spongy rolls with a sour cream topping.

2 packages active dry
  yeast
1 tablespoon honey
½ cup lukewarm water
1 cup milk
1 cup sour cream
2 tablespoons plus
  2 teaspoons corn oil
2 teaspoons sea salt
2 large eggs
1 cup wheat germ

6½ cups unbleached
  all-purpose flour
1 egg, slightly beaten with
  1 tablespoon water

TOPPING:
1 medium-sized onion,
  minced
3 tablespoons butter
½ cup sour cream
1 egg, slightly beaten
1 teaspoon onion powder
1 teaspoon kosher salt

Yield: 20 rolls

1. Combine yeast, honey and water in a small bowl. Set aside in a warm place until foamy and called for in recipe.
2. Heat milk until hot. Pour into a large mixing bowl.
3. Stir in sour cream, the 2 tablespoons corn oil, salt, eggs and wheat germ.
4. Mix in 2 cups flour.
5. Add foamy yeast. Mix.
6. Add 4 cups flour, 1 cup at a time, mixing well after each cup.

7. Knead last ½ cup flour into dough on table or board. Knead for about 5 minutes until dough is soft, smooth, light and non-sticky. (Do not add too much flour or dough will become heavy.)

8. Roll ball of dough in 1 teaspoon of the corn oil in bowl. Cover with a hot, damp towel and place bowl in sink filled with a few inches of hot water. Let dough rise until double in bulk, about 1 hour.

9. Punch dough down and roll in the remaining 1 teaspoon corn oil in bowl. Cover with a hot, damp towel and place in sink as before. Let dough rise for 30 minutes.

10. Divide dough into quarters, then divide each quarter into five equal pieces so that you have 20 pieces of dough in all.

11. Preheat oven at 375°F. Roll each piece of dough between the palms of your hands to form a ball and place on buttered baking sheet. Gently press down with your hand to slightly flatten each one. Cover with a dry towel and let rise until double in bulk, about 15 to 20 minutes.

12. While rolls are rising prepare topping. Sauté onion in butter until light golden brown, but do not over-cook. Put sautéed onion and its butter in a small bowl and stir in the remaining topping ingredients.

13. Brush tops of risen rolls with egg-water mixture and put about 1 teaspoon of the sour cream topping on each roll.

14. Bake for 25 minutes, or until rolls are golden brown, high and puffy on top, and sound hollow when tapped underneath.

15. Cool on wire racks.

Pizza

Most people are accustomed to the thin-crusted American pizza, but this is the thick-crusted Sicilian version.

DOUGH:
1 package active dry yeast
1 tablespoon honey
½ cup lukewarm water
1 cup milk
¼ cup butter
2 teaspoons sea salt
3 eggs
½ cup wheat germ
6 cups unbleached
  all-purpose flour
2 teaspoons corn oil for
  dough
9 tablespoons corn oil for
  pans

SAUCE:
6 tablespoons corn oil
6 cloves garlic, minced
6 (6-ounce) cans tomato
  paste
3 (6-ounce) cans water
Salt
Pepper
Oregano
Basil
1 (16-ounce) package
  mozzarella cheese
Pepperoni or anchovies
1 (12-ounce) container
  mushrooms, sliced
Grated Parmesan cheese
Olive oil

Yield: 3 large pizzas

1. To make the dough, combine yeast, honey and water in a small bowl. Set aside in a warm area until foamy and called for in recipe.
2. Heat milk until hot, letting butter melt in it. Pour into a large mixing bowl.
3. Stir in salt, eggs and wheat germ, then blend in 1 cup flour.
4. Mix in foamy yeast.
5. Add 4 cups flour, 1 cup at a time, mixing well after each cup.
6. Knead last 1 cup of flour into dough on table or board. Knead for about 15 minutes until dough is smooth, soft and very elastic. (Do not add too much flour or dough will be heavy; add just enough to make it non-sticky.)

7. Roll ball of dough in 1 teaspoon of the corn oil in bowl. Cover with clean towels and let rise in warm room until double in bulk, about 1½ hours.

8. Punch dough down and roll in the remaining 1 teaspoon corn oil in bowl. Cover and let rise for 30 minutes.

9. Punch down and form three balls of dough.

10. Put 3 tablespoons corn oil on each of three 10x15x 1-inch low-rimmed rectangular baking sheets, or any three fairly large baking sheets with low rims.

11. Spread oil all over inside surface of pans or baking sheets.

12. Preheat oven at 375°F. Very gently spread each of the three balls of dough on the oiled pans until it covers the width and length of the pan. If you feel confident enough you can throw the dough from palm to palm. This is an easier way to spread the dough. Press the dough into the four corners of each pan. Cover with a clean towel and let rise in warm room for 15 minutes. Bake for 10 minutes, then remove from oven.

13. Prepare sauce. Put 3 tablespoons of the corn oil in each of 2 large skillets. Put 3 cloves garlic into each skillet and sauté until light brown. Divide the tomato paste and water between the skillets.

Add salt, pepper, oregano and basil to taste to each skillet. Cook, stirring occasionally, over low heat for 20 minutes. (This makes a generous amount of sauce for three large pizzas.)

14. Spread the sauce over the three partially baked crusts.

15. Slice thin pieces of mozzarella and spread on top of each pizza.

16. Add thinly sliced pepperoni or anchovies.

17. Spread mushrooms on top.

18. Sprinkle with grated Parmesan cheese.

19. Sprinkle a little olive oil on top of each pizza.

20. Bake for 15 minutes. Serve hot.

Note: I usually bake one pizza and freeze the other two—after putting on the sauce and other ingredients —for later use. Then, when I'm ready to serve them I thaw them out for a few hours and bake for 15 minutes at 375°F.

Zeppoles (Italian Cakes)

Every Christmas my mother made *Julebrød,* in her
Norwegian tradition, and then she made *zeppoles,* in
my father's Italian tradition. My mother prepared the
dough and fried the cakes, while my father directed
the six of us, the children, in shaping the *zeppoles.* We
scrubbed down a huge wooden table until it was clean,
then scrubbed our hands and fingernails, sprinkled
flour on the table and began the long evening's work
of shaping an enormous batch of *zeppoles.* We were
always eager to eat the first fried *zeppoles* and barely
gave them a chance to cool. We filled huge crocks with
them and ate them for about two weeks.

I've eaten *zeppoles* at Italian festivals in New York
City, but they aren't nearly as good as these. Theirs are
made of plain dough, but ours is enriched with lots
of eggs and flavored with Parmesan cheese and anchovies.

This is a much smaller recipe than the one we used
to make.

Caution: Children can help to prepare the dough
and shape the *zeppoles,* but *an adult must do the frying. A pot of hot oil can be extremely dangerous. Keep
children away from pot of oil!*

2 packages active dry
    yeast
1 tablespoon honey
½ cup lukewarm water
2 cups milk
2 level teaspoons black
    pepper
1½ teaspoons sea salt
1 cup grated Parmesan
    cheese
1 cup wheat germ

5 tablespoons corn oil
9¼ cups unbleached
    all-purpose flour
7 large eggs, at room
    temperature
1 (13-ounce) can of flat
    anchovy fillets in olive
    oil with salt, drained
5 inches corn oil for deep
    fryer (about 2 quarts)

Yield: 50 to 60 *zeppoles*

1. Combine yeast, honey and water in a small bowl. Set aside in a warm place until foamy and called for in recipe.

2. Heat milk until hot and pour into a large mixing bowl.

3. Stir in pepper, salt, Parmesan cheese, wheat germ and 3 tablespoons of the corn oil.

4. Blend in 2 cups flour.

5. Add eggs, one at a time, beating with spoon for a few minutes after each addition.

6. Using a small knife, cut up anchovies into small pieces, and stir into batter.

7. Add 6 cups flour, 1 cup at a time, mixing well after each cup.

8. Knead last 1¼ cups flour into dough on table or board. (Try to use as little flour as possible for a soft but non-sticky dough. Too much flour makes a heavy *zeppole*.) Knead for 5 to 10 minutes.

9. Roll ball of dough in 1 tablespoon of the corn oil in bowl. Cover with a hot, damp towel and place bowl in sink with a few inches of hot water. Let dough rise until double in bulk, about 1 hour and 15 minutes.

10. Punch dough down and roll in the remaining 1 tablespoon corn oil in bowl. Cover with a hot, damp towel and place in sink as before. Let rise for 30 minutes.

11. While dough rises make preparations for frying *zeppoles*:

Pour 2 quarts corn oil into an electric deep fryer or a large pot on the stove. *Do not cover pot* while the oil is heating or there will be an explosion.

Let the oil heat to 375°F. in the electric fryer for 20 to 30 minutes. It must be very hot before frying the dough or the *zeppoles* will end up greasy.

Put several layers of paper towels on 4 large baking sheets or pans, for draining and cooling the *zeppoles*. (Do not put *zeppoles* on top of each other while draining or oil will seep into the ones below.)

12. After dough has risen for 30 minutes, cut off enough for a small loaf of bread. Roll it gently on a lightly floured table to form a long roll, about 10 inches long and 4 inches thick. Handle the dough as little as possible and use as little flour as possible if you want light, tender *zeppoles*.

13. Slice off small pieces of dough from the roll, each about 3 inches long and 1 inch thick. Using lightly floured hands roll each piece into a long strip, about 10 inches long and ½ inch thick or about long enough to form a big pretzel.

14. Shape the long strips into figure eights, closing the ends tightly. Let the *zeppoles* rise on the table for about 15 minutes before putting them into the hot oil.

15. Test the oil to see if it's hot enough. *Gently* drop a small piece of dough into the oil. If it rises almost immediately to the top of the oil and browns very quickly then the oil is hot enough.

16. Fry the risen *zeppoles*, 4 or 5 at a time, in very hot oil until golden brown on both sides. Turn only once, after bottoms of *zeppoles* have browned. To check if they're done, open up a cooled *zeppole*. If the dough inside is moist then you're not frying them long enough or the oil isn't hot enough or you made the *zeppoles* too fat. However, *zeppoles* are supposed to be slightly plump once they've puffed up in the hot oil. (Skinny *zeppoles* don't taste right.)

17. Remove *zeppoles,* one at a time, with long-handled perforated spoon, letting the oil drain back

into the pot before placing *zeppoles* on paper towels to drain.

18. Store loose *zeppoles* in crock, but put in plastic bags if storing in bread box to keep soft, when thoroughly cool (if you store them while still warm, they will mold). Do not refrigerate or they will dry out and harden. They taste better the next day when the Parmesan-anchovy flavor becomes stronger. *Zeppole* making is an art, and it takes practice to make really good, light, tender ones.

Note: If you wish to clarify the oil for later use, add a slice of peeled potato and let it cook for 15 to 20 minutes. The potato clarifies or "cleans" the oil.

Croissants

This is an easy recipe for delicious, light, very flaky croissants. It's a big recipe, making about 80 small croissants or about 60 regular ones. You can freeze half of the dough for use at another time if you don't wish to bake them all at once.

2 packages active dry
   yeast
1 tablespoon honey
½ cup lukewarm water
2 teaspoons sea salt
1½ cups warm milk
5½ cups unbleached
   all-purpose flour

2 eggs
1 tablespoon corn oil
2 pounds softened butter
1 egg yolk mixed with
   1 tablespoon milk

Yield: 80 small or 60 regular croissants

1. Combine yeast, honey and water in a small bowl. Set aside in a warm place until foamy and called for in recipe.
2. Put salt and milk into a large mixing bowl, stirring.
3. Blend in 2 cups flour.
4. Add eggs, beating for a few minutes with a spoon.
5. Mix in foamy yeast.
6. Blend in 3 cups flour.
7. Knead last ½ cup flour into dough on table or board. Knead only a few minutes. If you knead for too long the croissants will not be as flaky. Dough should be soft, smooth and elastic.
8. Roll ball of dough in corn oil in bowl. Cover with a clean towel and let rise in warm area until double in bulk, about 2 hours.
9. Punch dough down, and knead out any air bubbles.
10. Divide dough in half. Punch down one-half, cover with towels and set aside until ready to use. Take remaining half and roll it out with a rolling pin

on a lightly floured table to form a large rectangle about ¼ inch thick. Spread ½ pound butter on it, or cut butter into thin slices and place all over the dough. Fold dough over. Pinch seams tightly together so the butter doesn't come out. Roll out with a rolling pin to ⅛ inch thick. Spread ½ pound butter all over dough, fold over, seal seams tightly. Wrap loosely in a flour sprinkled sheet of aluminum foil and refrigerate for 2 or 3 hours. (Do not wrap in wax paper; it will stick to the dough.) Repeat process for other half of dough, using the remaining pound of butter. Chill in refrigerator a few hours or, if for use another day, place in freezer. When ready to use thaw for a few hours before preparing.

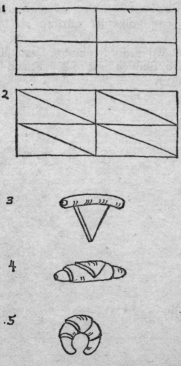

11. After dough has been chilled for a few hours, roll it out. Fold it over. Roll it out. Fold it over. Roll it out. Fold it over. Finally roll it out the fourth time to about ⅛ inch thick, to form a large rectangle. Using a knife, cut rectangle into squares. Divide squares in half to form triangles.

12. Roll up each triangle from the wide side. Press the tip of the triangle to the top middle of the roll.

13. Fold each roll inward to form a crescent shape. Place crescents, tip side down, on unbuttered baking sheets with *rims*. (Do not bake on rimless baking sheets or butter from croissants will drip onto floor of the oven.)

14. Cover pans of croissants with a dry cloth and let rise in warm area (but not on top of stove or butter will melt) for about 30 minutes. Preheat oven at 400°F.

15. Brush egg yolk-milk mixture on top of risen croissants.

16. Bake at 400°F. for 5 minutes. Drain off any excess butter in pan. Reduce heat to 350°F. and bake 8 to 10 minutes longer.

17. Cool on wire racks.

Egg Bagels

Bagels are easy to make. But they should be fairly small because they blow up to almost twice their size in the hot water.

2 packages active dry
   yeast
1 tablespoon honey
½ cup lukewarm water
1 cup hot milk
2 teaspoons sea salt
3 tablespoons plus
   1 teaspoon corn oil
½ cup wheat germ

5⅓ cups unbleached
   all-purpose flour
3 eggs
1 gallon water and
   1 tablespoon sugar
1 egg white mixed with
   1 tablespoon water
Sesame seeds

Yield: 24 bagels

1. Combine yeast, honey and water in a small bowl. Set aside in a warm area until foamy and called for in recipe.
2. Pour milk into a large bowl, and stir in the salt, the 3 tablespoons corn oil and wheat germ.
3. Blend in 1 cup flour.
4. Add 3 eggs, mixing well.
5. Mix in foamy yeast.
6. Add 4 cups flour, 1 cup at a time, mixing well after each cup.
7. Knead last ⅓ cup flour into dough on table or board. Knead for about 10 minutes to form a smooth, fairly stiff dough. (If dough hasn't enough flour, bagels may collapse after being boiled.)
8. Roll ball of dough in the 1 teaspoon corn oil in bowl. Cover with towels and place in sink filled with a few inches of hot water. Let dough rise until double in bulk, about 1 hour.
9. Punch dough down. Divide dough into 24 equal pieces, and roll each into a ball. Punch a hole in the center of each ball with a floured finger. Gently stretch bagels apart to enlarge holes. Place on ungreased

baking sheets, cover with a towel and let rise for about 15 minutes.

10. While bagels are rising, preheat oven at 375°F. Place a pot with 1 gallon water and 1 tablespoon sugar on the stove and bring to a boil.

11. When bagels have risen so that they are double in bulk, lower the heat under the pot of water so that the water simmers rather than boils. Place bagels, three at a time, in the water, turning after 3 minutes. Cook for 3 to 4 minutes on other side, turning only once for a total of 6 or 7 minutes.

12. Drain well on paper towels, and place bagels on ungreased baking sheets.

13. Bake for 10 minutes.

14. Brush egg white-water mixture on bagels and sprinkle with sesame seeds. Bake 20 to 25 minutes longer.

15. Cool on wire racks.

Sesame Rings

This is a yeast-raised version of Turkish sesame rings. The dough is very oily and easy to work with.

1 package active dry yeast
1 tablespoon honey
¼ cup lukewarm water
1 cup plain yogurt
1 cup corn oil

1½ teaspoons sea salt
5 cups unbleached
  all-purpose flour
1 egg
½ cup sesame seeds

Yield: 12 to 15 rings

1. Combine yeast, honey and water in a small bowl. Set aside in a warm place until foamy and called for in recipe.
2. Heat yogurt until very warm. Pour into a large mixing bowl.
3. Stir in corn oil, salt and 1 cup flour, blending thoroughly.
4. Mix in foamy yeast.
5. Add 3 cups flour, 1 cut at a time, mixing well after each cup.
6. Knead last 1 cup flour into dough on table or board to form a stiff but smooth and still somewhat oily dough. Knead for about 10 to 15 minutes. Place in bowl, cover with towels and let rise for 1 hour.
7. Punch dough down, return to bowl and let rise for 1 hour.
8. Cut off small pieces of dough, about the size of a tennis ball. Roll each piece into a thin 6-inch strip.
9. Slightly beat egg in a bowl. Place sesame seeds in another bowl.
10. Holding strip of dough at both ends with thumbs and forefingers, dip it into the egg and then into the sesame seeds until it is coated with seeds. Place on a buttered baking sheet. Shape strip into a circle and pinch ends together tightly. Let rise in a warm room until double in bulk, about 30 minutes. Preheat oven at 400°F.

11. Bake for 17 to 20 minutes.
12. Cool on wire racks.
13. Store thoroughly cooled sesame rings in plastic bags in bread box.

Soft Pretzels

This recipe makes 40 crusty, soft pretzels.

2 packages active dry
  yeast
3 tablespoons honey
½ cup lukewarm water
1 cup milk
1 cup water
¼ cup butter
2 teaspoons sea salt

7⅛ cups unbleached
  all-purpose flour
1 egg
1 teaspoon baking powder
2 teaspoons corn oil
1 egg white
Coarse salt

Yield: 40 thin, soft pretzels

1. Combine yeast, 1 tablespoon of the honey and lukewarm water in a small bowl. Set aside in a warm place until foamy and called for in recipe.
2. Heat milk, 1 cup water and butter in a small pot until hot. Pour into a large mixing bowl.
3. Add the remaining 2 tablespoons honey, salt and 2 cups flour, blending thoroughly.
4. Beat in the egg, then the foamy yeast.
5. Add baking powder and 2 cups flour, mixing well.
6. Add 2 more cups flour, 1 cup at a time, beating after each cup.
7. Knead last 1⅛ cups flour into dough on table or board. Knead 5 to 10 minutes until dough is firm, smooth and non-sticky.
8. Roll ball of dough in 1 teaspoon of the corn oil in bowl. Cover with towels and let rise for 1 hour.
9. Punch dough down and roll in the remaining 1 teaspoon corn oil in bowl. Cover bowl loosely with plastic wrap and refrigerate for 2 hours.
10. Divide dough into about 40 equal pieces, depending on how fat or thin you want the pretzels. Roll each piece on an unfloured table or board in a long, thin strip about 30 inches long and shape into pretzel, pinching ends together. Place on a buttered baking sheet and stretch it out. Cover with a towel and let rise about 15 minutes. Preheat oven at 400°F.

11. Brush tops of risen pretzels with egg white and sprinkle coarse salt on top. Be very sparing with salt.
12. Bake for 15 minutes.
13. Cool on wire racks.

Note: Many people dip their pretzel dough into a mild lye solution before baking, but I've never wanted to use lye on food and do not recommend it because it can be dangerous. So to get a similar characteristic pretzel flavor you can dissolve 1 tablespoon baking soda in a large pot containing 1 quart cold water and heat until steaming. Dip the pretzel rope into the soda solution for a second or two, then shape into pretzel, let rise and bake.

Index

ABOUT THE AUTHOR

MARY ANNE GROSS was raised in Yesterday's Village, New York, taught in elementary and junior high schools in New York City for eight years and now lives in Yesterday's Village with her husband, Angelo Ferraro, and their small daughter, Antonia. She is the author-editor of a children's book, *Ah, Man, You Found Me Again,* and is presently engaged in writing and illustrating other children's books. *Baking Bread the Way Mom Taught Me* is her first cookbook.

KITCHEN POWER!

☐	12207	**COOKING WITH HERBS AND SPICES** Craig Claiborne	$2.50
☐	11371	**SOURDOUGH COOKERY** Rita Davenport	$1.95
☐	13019	**MASTERING MICROWAVE COOKING** Scotts	$2.25
☐	12777	**PUTTING FOOD BY** Hertzberg, Vaughan & Greene	$2.95
☐	12278	**LAUREL'S KITCHEN** Robertson, Flinders & Godfrey	$3.95
☐	12263	**YOGURT COOKERY** Sophie Kay	$2.25
☐	11888	**CROCKERY COOKERY** Mable Hoffman	$2.25
☐	13168	**THE COMPLETE BOOK OF PASTA** Jack Denton Scott	$2.25
☐	13250	**MADAME WU'S ART OF CHINESE COOKING**	$2.25
☐	12186	**BETTER HOMES & GARDENS HOME** **CANNING COOKBOOK**	$1.95
☐	12979	**BETTY CROCKER'S COOKBOOK**	$2.50
☐	10538	**AMERICA'S FAVORITE RECIPES FROM** **BETTER HOMES & GARDENS**	$1.50
☐	12309	**THE ART OF FRENCH COOKING** Fernande Garvin	$1.75
☐	12199	**THE ART OF JEWISH COOKING** Jennie Grossinger	$1.95
☐	12316	**THE ART OF ITALIAN COOKING** Mario LoPinto	$1.75

Buy them wherever Bantam Bestsellers are sold or use this handy coupon:

Bantam Books, Inc., Dept. KP, 414 East Golf Road, Des Plaines, Ill. 60016

Please send me the books I have checked above. I am enclosing $_____
(please add 75¢ to cover postage and handling). Send check or money order
—no cash or C.O.D.'s please.

Mr/Mrs/Miss _____

Address _____

City _____ State/Zip _____

KP—9/79

Please allow four weeks for delivery. This offer expires 3/80.

KITCHEN POWER!

☐	11888	**CROCKERY COOKERY** Mable Hoffman	$2.25
☐	11107	**MICHEL GUERARD'S CUISINE MINCEUR** Michel Guerard	$2.50
☐	12857	**COOKING WITHOUT A GRAIN OF SALT** Elma Bagg	$2.25
☐	11782	**ART OF FISH COOKERY** Milo Milorandovich	$1.75
☐	2965	**THE ROMAGNOLIS' TABLE** The Romagnolis	$1.95
☐	12724	**THE WORLD-FAMOUS RATNER'S MEATLESS COOKBOOK** Judy Gethers	$1.95
☐	12215	**THE COMPLETE BOOK OF MEXICAN COOKING** Elisabeth Ortiz	$1.95
☐	13056	**THE FRENCH CHEF COOKBOOK** Julia Child	$2.75
☐	12107	**WHOLE EARTH COOKBOOK** Cadwallader & Ohr	$1.95
☐	13063	**BLEND IT SPLENDID: THE NATURAL FOODS BLENDER BOOK** The Dworkins	$1.95
☐	12512	**BETTY CROCKER'S DINNER FOR TWO**	$1.95
☐	11188	**BETTY CROCKER'S DINNER PARTIES**	$1.50
☐	11299	**THE SPANISH COOKBOOK** Barbara Norman	$1.50
☐	12908	**CREPE COOKERY** Mable Hoffman	$2.25

Buy them at your local bookstore or use this handy coupon for ordering:

Bantam Book Catalog

Here's your up-to-the-minute listing of over 1,400 titles by your favorite authors.

This illustrated, large format catalog gives a description of each title. For your convenience, it is divided into categories in fiction and non-fiction—gothics, science fiction, westerns, mysteries, cookbooks, mysticism and occult, biographies, history, family living, health, psychology, art.

So don't delay—take advantage of this special opportunity to increase your reading pleasure.

Just send us your name and address and 50¢ (to help defray postage and handling costs).